BEAUTY AS A STATE OF BEING

Mastering Mind and the Spiritual Path

DR. SOLOMON KATZ

A DEEPER CURRENTS BOOK

ISBN: 098911127X
ISBN 13: 9780989111270
Libary Congress Control Number: 2013920403
Deeper Currents Press
Harvard, Massachusetts

TABLE OF CONTENTS

dedicated to the love locked in every heart
waiting to be released

PREFACE

In a job interview at an institute for the integration of psychology and religion I was once asked, "Why have you gone outside your own religious tradition?" They knew my background: my parents were Holocaust survivors steeped in Orthodox Judaism. At the time of the interview, I practiced and supervised in clinical psychology at a teaching hospital affiliated with Harvard Medical School, and I had done my graduate work at Harvard in psychology and religion. The question referred to my experience prior to graduate school, when I lived as a Buddhist monk in Burma and Sri Lanka.

My answer was honest: I never really felt myself to be *anything* in particular. While I was a Buddhist monk I did not consider myself a Buddhist. I never felt that any label quite hit the mark: Jewish, Buddhist, American, human being. Yes, of course... but no, not exactly.

It turns out the sensibility I was describing is itself a religious tradition: *neti, neti* - not this, not this - the practice of negation rooted in the wisdom of India. This practice endorses my innate tendency to negate all self definitions. No label feels quite right for good reason: labels are always incomplete and thus inaccurate.

Eventually, through negation, you come to the fundamental reality that cannot be negated - Being itself - and *that* you are. But you arrive there only after dispensing with more superficial descriptions and identifications.

I bet the masters would agree. Great spiritual teachers try to point toward reality, freedom, eternity. The Buddha is not trying to create Buddhists. Christ is not trying to create Christians. Great teachers are interested in truth - call it God, Nirvana, Self-Realization - not in creating followers.

The great teachers, therefore, light the way. Because of my inclinations some teachings have rung truer than others, but this is a matter of taste as much as truth. Some teachings use language I am better able to understand, ideas with which I more deeply resonate, and so I am more deeply drawn there.

While I was raised in the Western traditions and could fluently read the Hebrew scriptures while sitting in an elementary school classroom, my primary influences are Eastern: Buddhism and the modern spiritual master, Ramana Maharshi, who died in 1950.

Ramana is becoming ever more widely recognized as a spiritual genius of the highest order. In the preface to <u>Talks with Ramana Maharshi,</u> Ken Wilber writes: "Talks... is the living voice of the greatest sage of the twentieth century and, arguably, the greatest spiritual realization of this or any time."

I completely agree. Ramana offers among the purest teachings ever expressed. For this reason, I will often quote from and use Ramana as a touchstone of truth.

A word about the structure and purpose of this book. This book aspires to be two things: a manual for mastering the mind so as to progress along the spiritual path, finding greater happiness along the way; and a work of art. As such, the book employs various styles of writing. Some chapters will carry the reader briskly along the spiritual path, as if you were on a bus tour covering the terrain carefully laid out in the itinerary, with the tour guide explaining all the sights as they pass. At other times the tour pauses; you spill out of the bus to browse the gift shop at a notable landmark. The forward movement then halts, and the writing changes from prose to something more like poetry to be browsed - and poetry will be interspersed with prose even in the forward moving chapters. My intent is to give the work greater power as a whole and, in the long run, greater clarity. But sometimes clarity takes time to simmer. My hope is for this book to stay with the reader, perhaps to be read more than once, perhaps to stay on the nightstand a while, or to be pulled off the shelf years after the initial reading.

Didactics

My friend the painter and teacher of painting once told me,
that an artist need not lay everything out in the most obvious terms.
Some mystery should to be retained - like the Mona Lisa -
some depth to ponder endlessly.
One purpose of art is to lead the viewer to depths,
that cannot be articulated;
depths that are beyond words, beyond the known.
But in *portraying* this unknown, the art offers access to it.
This is the didactics of art, its mode of instruction.

Yet another mode of instruction -
the didactics of science or philosophy, perhaps -
is to be as clear as possible;
to look into the ambiguous, glean clarity,
and then perfectly communicate the insight gained,
offering access to that same insight,
through a *perfectly* articulated map,
a precise formula that everyone can follow,
leaving little to misunderstanding.

We tread here, dear reader, the tension,
between the didactics of clarity,
and the didactics of mystery.

CHAPTER 1

MIND

My colleague and I work in the field of mental health. I work as a psychologist, she works as a psychiatric nurse practitioner, and we work together in a practice that we share. Recently I was talking to her about a patient that I was seeing. She asked, "What is his diagnosis?" I was inclined to answer, "He has the same diagnosis as everyone else that I see: He has a mind." Or I could have elaborated: "He takes his thoughts seriously. He is embedded in his thoughts. He believes the conversation going on in his head is significant." That is his - and everyone's - diagnosis.

Clinical diagnoses like anxiety or depression describe different patterns of mind, different ways the mind may spin. Or the therapeutic focus might involve self-esteem, self-image, or self-doubt; other ways the mind may spin. The mind spins in many ways and its different preoccupations create different emotional disturbances. But the bottom line, the universal diagnosis is always, "He or she has a mind and it is spinning."

There is a slogan that says, "A mind is a terrible thing to waste." Yes, but a mind can also be a terrible thing. Obsessing with worry, fear, anxiety, depression, all the forms of unhappiness - these are products of the mind. The conflict in the world - anger, violence and war - these are also products of the mind.

Having a mind is overrated. It needs to be used well or, possibly, not at all. Then there may be peace.

Power Tool

The mind is like a power tool, a chainsaw, for example. A chainsaw is very helpful when used for the purposes for which it is designed. We heat our home with wood in the winter, and the seven cords of firewood seasoning all summer in the yard would hardly be possible without a good chainsaw. But the chainsaw must be used properly and according to purpose or it can wreak havoc. The mind too is powerful and capable of extraordinary creativity and invention but, when used improperly, can become an instrument of personal and global undoing.

Fingers and Buttons

Most people call a psychologist when they are in turmoil. But what, really, is the problem? Certainly the affairs of life may be in turmoil. There may be a crisis in personal relationships like loneliness or divorce. There may be a job or financial loss, especially in times of economic distress. There may be physical illness. But it is imaginable that someone even facing death may be perfectly at peace - or he may be in a panic.

Unhappiness is a result of inner turmoil not necessarily an outer situation. The outer situation puts pressure on the mind, pushes its buttons. But if the buttons do not get pushed, if there is no inner spinning, the mind can remain at peace even when faced with crisis.

The Indian sage, Nisargadatta, has said, "Life is full of rings; make straight your hooks." If there are no hooks there is no place for the rings that life throws to catch. I sometimes say more prosaically, "Life is full fingers; get rid of your buttons."

In life there is no shortage of fingers trying to push your buttons. That is perhaps one of life's purposes - to push your buttons, to point out which buttons remain, where you are still vulnerable, where your mind is still capable of going into a spin. Do not worry when life fulfills its purpose of nudging, maybe shoving you in the direction of your confusion for the sake of its enlightenment. Your job is to dismantle your buttons. When no buttons remain no reactivity remains; inner confusion - mind - has largely been dismantled and underlying peace prevails.

Balance

An infant learning to walk must discover the point of balance. Balance is not known at first - there are many disappointing falls onto the benevolent cushion of the diaper - but must be discovered and mastered through trial and error.

When the infant grows into a young child and learns to ride a bicycle, she must similarly discover the point of balance. When she first tries to ride the bicycle the point of balance is not known, it must be discovered. Once found, however, the point of balance becomes familiar and the joys of cycling open. But when she loses her balance while either walking or cycling - say she slips on ice while walking, or skids on sand while cycling - a tremendous sense of unease and discomfort arises and she urgently tries to right herself, so terribly uncomfortable is the loss of balance. Balance is bliss, while the loss of balance is disarray and panic.

Spiritually speaking, we are all like children trying to find the point of balance. This holds true both for the individual trying to find personal happiness, and for society trying to find peace among men and women, and nations. Like a child learning to walk or cycle, the point of existential balance - balance in life - is not known until discovered. But once discovered it too is characterized by bliss. Balance - whether walking, cycling, or traversing life - feels intuitively *right* while imbalance feels wrong and is a state of personal and social suffering.

Symptoms

When you lose your balance there is an immediate feeling of discomfort. The discomfort is feedback from the organism that something is awry. The discomfort is a *symptom* of the loss of balance and onset of disequilibrium.

Let's say you are driving in the right lane on the highway and are perfectly balanced in the center of the lane. You are in *the very heart* of the lane. You are balanced; swaying neither to the right nor to the left and all is well.

Then you lose focus and start to veer right. You are no longer centered but are veering off course. But the grooves on the side of the highway rumble your tires and awaken you to the fact that you are off balance and approaching danger.

The grooves are like symptoms, feedback from the road that you have lost the center. The feedback urges you to get back on track quickly before you end up hitting the guard rail, with even more dramatic symptoms that things have gone terribly wrong.

Physical or emotional symptoms, subtle and gross, similarly indicate that something is awry. When you are centered in the heart, joy, peace, and illumination prevail and all is right with the world. When there is some deviation from the heart, symptoms of discomfort arise as feedback from the organism. The symptom is your friend, as it alerts you to the fact that balance has been lost and a redress is necessary. The heart must be recovered for peace to be restored. For the heart is radiant Being and intuitively the place where all is truly well.

The Chiropractics of the Soul

Before he had surgery my friend Jamie's shoulder often dislocated. We would be playing softball and the game would have to stop. Andy, who was skilled in yoga and body mechanics, would run over to help. When Jamie's shoulder came out of joint he would be in great pain. When Andy got the arm reinserted into the shoulder socket, Jamie's pain was relieved and the game would go on. Thankfully, surgery provided a long-term solution to the problem.

In the same way, we suffer emotionally when the mind is out of joint. Just as symptoms of physical pain signal physical disturbance, symptoms of emotional pain signal mental disturbance. But, as with the bad shoulder, when everything internal is back in place the fountain of happiness flows. Unhappiness is an indication that the mind is out of joint, that some truth remains unseen.

For this reason, I sometimes refer to the psychological or spiritual work as "the chiropractics of the soul." A chiropractor tries to line the body up, to relieve the impingement that is causing pain. When the spine is straight, in place, when no nerves are pressed upon, energy flows freely and pain disappears. In the psychological or spiritual domain, when the "soul" is properly aligned suffering disappears.

This implies, again, that peace and happiness are the natural condition. Unhappiness is only a symptom of misalignment, inner disturbance calling for attention. When the soul is properly aligned happiness reappears - the state of balance to which we all aspire.

The Heart and the All

Let's consider the word "soul" for a moment. What does "soul" actually mean?

I like the following definition, a definition consistent with Indian philosophy and which has parallels in most spiritual traditions. Indian philosophy proposes that *Atman is Brahman*: the indwelling spirit (Atman) is, in fact, the Absolute (Brahman).* The individual soul is the same thing as the universal soul. In other words, your essence, the most intimate aspect, the very heart of your being is the universal Being, the Eternal, the All. The soul, then, is the Heart and the All. At heart, you are literally God. The most intimate heart is, paradoxically, vast.

I will say more about this later. It is not necessary to accept this premise in order to progress in our primary purpose of peace and well-being. I will show the rationale for this perspective and that it has been affirmed by many spiritual traditions.

For now, this point of view suggests that, if you find your core, usually through some form of meditation, you sink below the definitions and limitations of mind and come to know yourself as expansive and undefined. As it has been said, God hid in the hearts of men and women knowing this would be the last place they would look. Or as Ramana Maharshi has said, "After finding who you are, you may see what God is."

*(The Sage) is established in an undifferentiated state where the Atman, having realized its identity with the Brahman, shines of its own light. (Klein, Jean. Be Who You Are. P. 40).

Quiet

Inner spinning - busyness of mind - is agitation. Agitation is the opposite of peace; peace is the absence of agitation. Since peace is the absence of agitation, for there to be inner peace agitation must subside. The mind must become quiet. When the mind is quiet peace is revealed, for peace is that very quiet.

When the mind is "in joint" it causes no disturbance; it is quiet. It is like the power tool used well, according to purpose, and only when needed. (You don't keep the chainsaw running in the living room all day). There is no anxiety, no depression, no thought of fear or failure which is mind *out* of joint. If you pay careful attention the conversation in your head is uncomfortable, noisy, a disturbance of peace, like static disturbing an otherwise clear signal; feedback from the organism that mind is off course and needs to be *reoriented to the heart.*

The Thinker is the Thought

The philosopher, J. Krishnamurti, has said, "The thinker is the thought... there is no thinker separate from thought." This means that the thought spoken in your own voice creates the sense of the one doing the speaking: the ego. The thinker arises with and is part-and-parcel of the thought spoken in his or her own voice. So the thinker - the ego - is equivalent to the thought process. No thinking, no ego. The ego vanishes with the vanishing of thought but *you* as Being remain, the source from which mind and ego have arisen, and its nature is peace.

Review

Let's review; there will be flash quiz coming! When you first learn to ride a bicycle, you must discover what balance feels like; you do not know the feeling of balance at first. But once you discover the point of balance, it feels very comfortable. You say to yourself, "Oh, I see,

I've got it now. Nice." We can call this point of balance the heart, the perfect center. Any loss of balance feels immediately uncomfortable and there is an instinctive tendency to correct the imbalance before it gets worse. The more unbalanced you are, the more uncomfortable.

When your body is healthy, when the chiropractics are lined up correctly, there is similarly a feeling of wellness and happiness. But if something goes out of alignment, if you break your arm, for example, symptoms of pain arise to indicate that something is broken. The organism intuitively knows what wellness should feel like, what it feels like *not* to be broken, so when there is physical or emotional discomfort, when symptoms arise, you intuitively know that something is wrong. Something is out of whack.

The natural existential condition is a state of balance but, like riding a bicycle, this condition must be discovered. Once discovered, it feels intuitively right. In this state *everything* - the soul - is properly aligned. You are centered in your heart. There is a spontaneous feeling of wellness, happiness, joy, peace, and generosity of spirit. The mind is quiet, causing no disturbance.

Deviating from this condition occurs with the arising of mind. This is the arising of the ego, the one doing the talking in his or her own voice. With the arising of mind, quiet is lost. The more that quiet is lost, that is, the busier the mind becomes, the more agitated you feel as you drift away from the peace of the heart. You feel increasingly off balance and uncomfortable. At first subtle and later gross symptoms arise the more off center you drift, the more the mind spins, the crazier the mind becomes, with inappropriate behavior to follow. Now you are bouncing off the guard rail! You might start acting inappropriately, getting panicky, getting angry, drinking, suppressing symptoms one way or another to avoid their discomfort. But the real solution is found only in correcting course, returning the mind to quiet, abandoning the inner spinning, and steering back to center where balance and the heart are recovered. The symptoms are feedback from your organism - from life - that you have lost balance, lost the heart, and need to correct course in order to recover the happiness that is naturally characteristic of the heart.

Nuts

The mind is a wonderful tool when used for the purposes for which it is well suited. When used appropriately the mind is silent and invisible. Mind simply serves as a channel for the Innate Creativity of the heart (See Movie Projector, in the next chapter). The mind is able to use language, balance the checkbook, design the architecture of buildings, cities and computers, do mathematics and physics, compose masterpieces in books, symphonies, and the visual arts. The mind is expressed in each academic department in the university and in every field of knowledge.

When oriented to the heart, mind serves the purposes of Innate Creativity and is invisible, a non-issue. We are not concerned about mind in this capacity, the power tool used appropriately. We are concerned about mind in the sense of ego. The ego is the voice in your head, the talking in your head, the inner conversation that creates the illusion of a personal self, the guy or gal in there who is doing the talking. But the ego is an illusion (also discussed in the next chapter) that is created by, that is *equivalent* to the inner conversation. No conversation, no ego. With each thought, with each moment of scintillating conversation you have with yourself, you are reaffirming the personal self, the ego. Yet it is this same conversation that drives you totally nuts.

The price of the conversation you have with yourself, the price of the ego is to be nuts. The personal mind is *by definition* nuts, is *synonymous* with nuts. If you have a mind/ego, you're nuts. And the louder the conversation, the denser the thicket of mind, the more nuts one is, the more severe the diagnosis.

I often say that everyone walking in my office door does so because their mind is driving them crazy. Everyone is crazy to the degree of the inner spinning, the conversation of the personal self. Sanity is a quiet mind; mind oriented to heart.

In order to find sanity, the personal conversation must return to quiet for it only obscures the very thing you are seeking: silence, the *source* of the conversation, the heart, your very *Self.*

The mind used appropriately is a great evolutionary advance. But the ego/mind is perhaps like the appendix: a vestigial organ that will be disposed of once we, as a species, evolve to discover the deeper truth of the heart. The heart will then manifest fully in the individual and collective life. The heart will someday rule the earth.

The Map

How to find the heart? Every journey requires a good map. It puts the journey into perspective, conveys some sense of what lies ahead, how long the journey might take, and what to expect along the way.

It is important, though, that the map, the drawing of the terrain, is an accurate representation of the terrain it attempts to draw. If the map is not accurate but I follow it nevertheless, taking it to be true, I will not end up where I expect. If, for example, my map tells me to go north from Boston to arrive in California, I will be very surprised when I find myself in Canada instead, and the weather is not the warm weather I wanted, but is actually much colder than where I left.

Many world views - religious, philosophic, political - may not be accurate representations of the truth, bad maps. Yet these maps - these purported descriptions of life-truth and the direction of paradise - are followed with fervent belief. But bad maps do not accurately point the way. As a result the world ends up in conflict, not in sunny climates at all, not closer to peace but farther away. Consider, then, whether the map you follow actually leads to universal peace and happiness.

We can speculate at this point that *happiness is the measure and compass of truth*. When things are untrue, out of joint, there is pain; when the chiropractics of the soul are in place, the fountain of happiness flows. Happiness is the compass that points toward and indicates the presence of truth, both for the individual and the collective, the world as a whole. This has implications for the way we conduct ourselves personally and politically. The course that is consistent with the nature of things should bring about personal and universal happiness.

We can further speculate that the very purpose of this world, this earth, is to point toward spiritual truth through the mechanism of suffering and its relief. Through living in the world, searching for happiness, we discover what does and what does not work. We may have to try every falsity first, worship at the altar of every pretension, until we recognize the truth that actually works.

I would like to propose a simple map for our journey:

First there is Negative-thinking.

Better than that is Positive-thinking.

Better still is No-thinking.

As we will see, this map encompasses virtually all psychological and spiritual methods prescribed through the ages for the journey that begins with suffering and ends with peace. Again:

First there is Negative-thinking.

Better than that is Positive-thinking.

Better still is No-thinking.

Metaphors

I have a weakness for metaphors (as might already be apparent!) but want my metaphors to clarify rather than confuse. So, before proceeding with the map, let me try to preempt any confusion by pointing out the essential principle that most metaphors represent: *the heart and the deviation from the heart into mind.* The heart is the center, the point of balance, inner peace and stillness, the creative source, the Self. Deviating from this source is the arising of mind, but mind not as a channel for the expression of Innate Creativity - the best use of mind - but mind as ego, the conversation of the personal self which is agitated, nuts, the power tool used badly, described below using the Buddhist term of *craving.*

Flash Quiz: Equations

ego = mind = thinking

Self = Heart = Innate Creativity

Obsessing about your Dilemma

Another, most elegant map for the spiritual journey was presented twenty five hundred years ago by the Buddha. After the Buddha attained enlightenment, he began his teaching of the path to enlightenment by proclaiming the Four Noble Truths, the essential doctrine of Buddhism.

The Buddha's map, the Four Noble Truths are:

1. Life is fraught with Suffering
2. There is a cause of suffering: Craving.
3. There is an end to suffering: Nirvana.
4. There is a path to the end of suffering: The Eightfold Path.

The Four Noble Truths deserves many books on its own. I mention it here to make just one point.

The cause of suffering is usually translated as "craving." Craving suggests that suffering is caused by a psychological behavior - or mis-behavior - that creates disequilibrium.

Craving is usually interpreted as follows. Where I am at any given moment is not exactly where I want to be. I want something else; something better or different. The present moment always seems insufficient. I want something that I do not now have, and what I have I do not entirely want. I am restless, ill at ease in my existence.

When the stars do line up in a period of good fortune, I may be happy for the moment because I have what I want. But springtime and romance do not last forever. Eventually circumstances change, the good fortune passes, and I am back to wondering what went wrong.

While craving is a term often used to represent the Second Noble Truth, the cause of suffering, I like to use the phrase, "Obsessing about your dilemma." To crave is to be in a state of wanting what you do not have. "Obsessing about your dilemma" is similarly to be preoccupied with the story line of your life, what is *wrong* with the story at the moment, what needs to happen in the future for desire to be fulfilled and happiness ensue, because the present is deemed insufficient. The cause of suffering, then, is this state of obsessing about your dilemma: mind/ego in perpetual motion.

I was in New York City recently with my family. We had a good weekend and it was time to drive home. We checked out of the room, I drove the car up and we loaded the bags into the trunk. But there was one more errand that needed to be done and, rather than find another parking space in New York, I parked alongside a hydrant and waited with the car while the gang had fun.

I had fun of a different sort. I sat in the car and watched people walk by. It was as if I could see each person thinking, wrapped up in her thoughts, mulling over the situation at hand, what was happening and what needed to be done.

Everyone, it seems, is walking around obsessing about her dilemma. There is almost always a situation that needs pondering and improving. It is rare that one walks around attuned to wonder.

Obsessing obscures wonder. If I place my hand just in front of my face, my small hand obscures the vast horizon. Obsessing is so up front, so prominent, that it obscures a more panoramic view of life. In order to attune to wonder, obsessing - preoccupation with the personal self and the dilemma du jour - must stop. What dilemma have you been obsessing about lately? What dilemma is in the background even as you read these words? Stop obsessing and be still - *you dwell in eternity.* (More on eternity in Chapter VII).

Years ago when my daughter was quite young, she asked, "Daddy, *where* are we? I mean, I know we're in Massachusetts, I know we're on the earth, but where is any of it, really? Where are we?"

I gave my best answer. "Sweetheart, we are in Consciousness. Everything is Consciousness. Let's say at night, from your bed in Massachusetts, you dream that you are in New York. But your experience of New York was really only in your imagination. You were in your bed all the time! Whatever took place in your dream was located in your mind, nowhere else. This world is also like a dream in your awareness. That is where everything is located: in Consciousness." But I could equally have said, "Sweetheart, we are in eternity. We are literally in the middle of nowhere."

Fundamentally, mind - the business of obsessing - is the real dilemma. You, as an ego, are the voice in your head and the voice in your head is the sound that obsessing makes. You could be at the Grand Canyon and still the sound would continue, barely allowing for an appreciation of the vista below. In a sense you are perpetually at the Grand Canyon - in eternity, in mystery - but obsessing and dilemma obscure that.

When I stop practicing as a psychologist, I will leave a note on my door for anyone who comes by. The note will contain the wisdom I have gleaned in my years of practice and my instructions for any would-have-been patients. The note will say, "Don't Obsess!"

So: No thinking, no mind. No mind, no problem!

Nirvana

One more word about the Buddha's Four Noble Truths. According to the Four Noble Truths the end of suffering is Nirvana. It is not winning the lottery. It is not winning the Super Bowl. It is not getting tenure. It is not getting the girl. The end of suffering is not found in getting what you want but in *not wanting*. Because desire - craving - is agitation. The end of suffering is about the stilling of agitation, finding happiness not without in a quest for objects, but within as the very nature of the radiant heart, the Self. It is finding happiness not in the fulfillment of desire but in the absence of desire. We will say more about this later.

From this perspective it is still possible to pursue the fulfillment of desire, but from a position of non-attachment; happiness does not depend on desires being fulfilled. If they are fulfilled, great, if not that too is okay because you are already anchored in the radiant heart and the fulfillment of desire is icing on the cake. The radiant heart is the nature of Being, prior to the fulfillment or frustration of any desire.

It is said, after attaining enlightenment, that the Buddha was moved by compassion to teach. He saw humanity seeking happiness in ways that were certain to preclude the happiness that was being sought. Happiness was sought primarily in objects and not within as *a state not a circumstance.*

Also: The Four Noble Truths is a map, not a religion. Religions arise once the mind gets hold of a sage's teaching and adds on hats and fruit - all kinds of ritual complexity that confuses more than clarifies the teaching.

Spiritual teachings are like directions. You've never been to Boston? Alright, from here go east on Route 2, drive about 45 minutes, get onto Storrow Drive, that will take you into Boston.

You want to find the end of suffering? Alright, says the Buddha in the Fourth Noble Truth, the path to the end of suffering. First clarify your outer life through ethical conduct.* Clean up any messes in your outer life. It is hard to find inner peace when your outer life is a mess. Then clarify your inner life through meditation. Purify your mind. Get your mind back in joint where it is silent and subservient. Once there is clarity in the outer and inner worlds you will recognize the radiant heart, always present but obscured by all the mess. That is the direction of Nirvana.

Spiritual teachings, like directions to Boston, are offered by masters who have found their way to Boston (or the Metro area - any teaching that may contribute to the relief of suffering) and are just making shorter work of the trip. Anyone would gladly do the same. No need for a hat, skip the fruit.

But following directions requires faith. When I ask directions of someone, I get a sense whether they know what they're talking about or not. If I sense they know the way, I follow their directions and end up at my destination. Though I may never have been to Boston, or to the end of suffering, in order to begin the journey I must have the faith that the directions I am being given are accurate and will lead me there.

The Buddha begins with the obvious: life is fraught with suffering. But he goes on to say that suffering can be ended and it can be ended by taking certain steps. I mention this for those who deeply doubt or are deeply skeptical. Have a little faith. The brilliant day ahead is not always apparent in the dim light and mist of early morning.

*Specifics regarding ethical conduct and ways to keep the outer life in order will be given in Chapter V.

Birthday

As I blew out the birthday candles,
I made my wish for grace - spiritual and worldly,
and that job would be especially nice, like frosting on the cake.
The world is frosting on the cake;
Self is enough (*dayenu*),
but on top of Self has been added a buttercream world.
While Self may be enough it is also true,
within the world, the realm of gain and loss,
that gain feels a whole lot better than loss,
up better than down days in the market for the sundry goods of life.
In the stock market bull is better than bear;
in the job market yes is better than no;
even with weather:
better today when the sun broke through,
than the clouds comeuppance when the cold wind blew.

Sometimes it may seem that gain, success, the answer yes,
would heal every ill;
but truer to say that Self is enough and *Peace is in Every Moment.*
The I that was born would like the job, a bundle of cash, sunny days.
To the I that was never born, it does not matter at all.

The Climate of Your Psyche

He is very unhappy in his marriage, will separate soon and probably divorce. As is often the case, there is someone else in the background and they spent a day at the beach last week. He thinks he will be much happier with this other person. I'm not sure it will make that much difference in the long run.

You live in the climate of your psyche and your psyche goes with you from one relationship to the next. Happiness is not found simply by moving the pieces on the chessboard of life. Usually happiness is sought by trying to change situations for the better. But if happiness is "a state not a circumstance" then changing circumstances, even when appropriate, does not address the issue of happiness at its root.

There is an often told story: a man at night is searching the ground under a streetlight. His friend comes by and asks: "What's the matter?" The man replies: "I'm looking for my keys." "Where did you lose them?" "Way over there." "Then why are you looking here?" "Well, there's no light over there!"

You can look and look but if you are looking in the wrong place the keys will never be found. If happiness is sought only by changing circumstances it will never be found, because you are looking in the wrong place. If you bring a disorganized mind into a new set of circumstances you will still experience a disorganized mind. New circumstances may indeed be preferable, a genuine improvement, but some part of the problem is not solved. Only by finding inner truth, only by resolving internal confusion can abiding happiness be realized.

I would suggest "Thou shalt have no gods before Me," means *for your own good*: "Have no gods, no preoccupations, no thoughts before Me." Stay attentive. Release your preoccupations. The end of suffering is found not through more and more thinking in an attempt to resolve the dilemma, but in the cessation of thinking, bringing mind and dilemma to rest. Then the radiance, obscured by all the busyness, will emerge. The end of suffering, says the Buddha, is Nirvana, the proper alignment of the soul.

Mastery

One more balance metaphor before we move on. An expert skier, a ski jumper, can literally soar through the air and land comfortably on his skis hundreds of meters down the mountain. He is able to hold the point of balance even under very challenging circumstances. A mogul skier can remain balanced and upright even while racing the big bumps. The challenge is viewed not as an occasion for panic but as great fun, a thrill. To a novice skier, however, gathering even a little speed on the bunny slope can be an occasion for panic; that relatively minor circumstance may cause a loss of balance and ungainly tumble.

When there is some mastery, when the mind is comfortable, quiet and non-reactive, properly aligned and "in joint," when you have deeply found the point of existential balance - *your heart* - apparently challenging circumstances need not cause distress but are viewed, rather, as bumps in the terrain that may actually add enjoyment and humor to the skiing. From this perspective, life is a great miracle here to serve the edification of the soul - and to thrill.

CHAPTER II

NEGATIVE-THINKING

Q: How to avoid misery?
A: Has misery a shape? Misery is only unwanted thought. The mind is not strong enough to resist it. (Talks with Ramana Maharshi. P. 156)

When Ramana Maharshi is asked, "How to avoid misery?" he responds, "Has misery a shape?" Is misery an object that one can avoid? Misery is only unwanted thought. Misery *is* your wayward thought process, nothing more. No wayward thought, no misery. The mind is simply not strong enough to withstand its negative tendencies and misery results. So we need to strengthen the mind. A strong mind is a stable mind, able to hold the point of balance even under challenging circumstances.

Heaven and Hell

I have often wondered why, simultaneously,
nature can reflect such beauty,
outwardly there can be so great an appearance,
of beauty and harmony,
yet inwardly the state of the body and mind,
can diverge so dramatically from that outward appearance.
While the outer world manifests perfection -
billowing clouds in an azure sky, gentle breezes, bird songs -
the body and mind can be in a state of subtle or utter disarray,
a capsule of disharmony,
emotional confusion and physical pain.
And somehow, ironically,
it is this capsule of hell that gazes out toward that heaven.

The Unrestrained Mind

As suffering is the point of departure for the Four Noble Truths, negative thinking is the point of departure for our journey. If there were
no negative thinking and its consequent unhappiness, there would be
no need for a map or a journey.

There are two kinds of negative thinking related to: 1) the process
of mind and, 2) the content of mind.

Negative thinking with regard to the *process* of mind refers to the
activity of mind regardless of the content of thought. Negative process
is a mind that is disorderly, wayward, out of control. Imagine that you
are riding a horse but have no reins to hold, no control over the animal.
You are completely at its mercy. You go helplessly where it goes, in the
direction it goes, at the speed it goes, for as long as it goes. If the horse

wants to gallop all night, then you gallop all night and forego sleep. If the horse turns this way or that, you turn with it. The process of the unrestrained mind is negative simply because it is unrestrained.

I remember hearing a researcher on National Public Radio talk about the brain in the process of decision making. He confessed that he could be in the cereal aisle at the supermarket and struggle inwardly with the different cereals and box sizes, trying to make the right choice. Should he buy Honey Nut Cheerios or Frosted Cheerios? Original Cheerios or Multi-Grain? The smaller box or the bargain size? While there is nothing negative in the content of his thinking - the relative merits of *Cheerio*'s, after all - the process, the excessive activity of mind is itself tiresome. It is hard for a mind this busy to go off-duty; it never punches out; it stays on the job at all hours and sleep may be hard to come by.

The galloping horse represents the mind that has deviated from the state of stillness into agitation. Another classic metaphor for the mind in a state of peace, and then the deviation into agitation, is that mind is like water. The inherent nature of water is to be still and clear. But when the winds blow the waters roil. Water is not naturally opaque; it is only opaque when agitated. Remove the agitation and the water will return to its natural state of stillness and clarity. The mind too is by nature still and clear but churns when agitated. Negative process indicates a mind that is agitated regardless of the reason. It could even be Cheerios!

Distraction

The sole cause of man's unhappiness is that he does not know how to stay quietly in his room. (Pascal, Pensees).

The galloping horse represents the mind that runs and runs, the mind that is always busy. When it runs rampant your mind becomes a burden. How often have I been asked, "Is there some switch I can flip to turn it off?" The only relief seems to be in medication or distraction. I often suggest reading, especially spiritual, high-vibration reading, as a respite from the relentlessly busy mind. While reading, the mind is engaged and the galloping is restrained. The mind settles into the reading and becomes tame. In fact, reading works much like meditation, as we will see, in that attention is given a focus and agitation is subdued into focus. This is the case whenever we are engaged in a meaningful or exciting activity, like travel, a great conversation, playing sports, playing music. The mind is absorbed into the activity, its focus, and becomes invisible.

Work acts in much the same way. The mind is occupied while working and work is usually quite healthy. I have observed that when people receive disability benefits and are freed from the financial requirement to work, they become less happy and their lives often deteriorate. Because there is no need to work, there is no reason to get out of bed in the morning, and the emptiness of schedule is filled with an inflation of thinking.

If I remember correctly from college, Sartre wrote a play, "No Exit," where hell was being trapped with other people for eternity.

In fact, hell is being trapped with your own mind without distraction. The most brutal punishment we inflict is solitary confinement. Yet there are monks, nuns, and contemplatives who willingly seek out isolation. When you know how to navigate your inner being, how to bring the mind to subsidence, there is the potential for inner peace. Absent this knowledge, being left alone with one's mind is considered torture.

So the world is occupied with distraction. Work consistently enough, leave no gaps, seek entertainment when not working, watch plenty of TV, movies, or video games, consume plenty of alcohol or other substances on weekends, maybe go to the casino, and it is possible to distract yourself sufficiently from the solitary confinement of being trapped with yourself. Until the time when you see the futility of distraction, or can no longer avoid the pull of the heart and so willingly engage the problem. You choose to look directly at rather than avoid the demon, and see there was no demon there at all.

Negative Content: The Taste Test

Every thought in the personal conversation - the process of a distracted mind - has a "taste," an emotional flavor. Some thoughts taste better than others. Thinking about your children generates love and brings a smile to your face. Thinking about your boss generates, well...

There are two sides to each thought: the verbal content and its associated emotional flavor. So, depending on the nature of the internal conversation, one emotional experience or another is generated. If

you think about the plunging stock market and your dwindling retirement funds, you become despondent and life seems like an ordeal.
Such is the taste of that contemplation. If you are having marital
problems, you may be focused on the resentment left from the many
hurts of the past. If you are captured by white clouds drifting across
a blue sky, that contemplation will leave a sense of well-being. If you
look carefully at any plant, you may feel touched by its innocence and
goodwill. The beauty of nature will often generate joy; fretting about
money will generate anxiety. It is important to be aware of your inner
focus, the contemplation of the moment, because that contemplation
creates the mood of experience.

Earlier we discussed negative *process* regardless of the content of
thought. But negative *content* involves thoughts with a bitter taste and
painful effect on the psyche. Negative thoughts may involve anger,
hatred, frustration, blame, failure, regret, criticism, annoyance, impa-
tience, irritability, disappointment, sadness, despair, boredom, inad-
equacy, doubt, fear, worry, envy, self pity, arrogance, self-importance
and so on. Quite a selection to choose from!

If you persist in negative thoughts you will become ill. Just as a
steady diet of junk food will make you ill, a steady stream of negative
thoughts will do the same. Negativity is toxic. So be sensitive to the
taste of your thoughts, because each thought flavors the psyche in
some way. Avoid the mental junk food.

If you bit into a rotten tomato you would spit it out immediately.
The bad taste tells you that the food is rotten and consuming it will

make you ill. If you ignored the bad taste and persisted in eating the rotten tomatoes, eventually your body would rebel and regurgitate the toxicity altogether. Yet in the domain of thought, where taste is subtle and not so readily apparent, we may consume one bad thought tomato after another. Symptoms of illness eventually develop; so tainted has the mind and spirit become.

As you worry you create anxiety. Each worried thought only deepens the mood of anxiety. Once anxiety has become symptomatic, you may worry even about worrying! If there has been one panic attack, any worry about a future panic attack only adds fuel to the fire. Each worried thought takes you precisely in the wrong direction. To avoid further anxiety change the focus entirely; try contemplating love. Take some time, for example, and think of every person you have loved in the course of your life: parents, classmates, friends, best friends, your first love, all the subsequent great loves, your spouse, your children, your clients. Feel appreciation for those with whom you have shared your life journey, and see how your mood changes. This is an example of Positive-thinking.

In a sense you are always in contemplation, but what are you contemplating? You might be contemplating the beauty of nature, love and appreciation for your friends, or just what a bum your husband is. Be careful. Choose the object of your contemplation carefully; whether it is of contempt or whether of grace.

Anxiety is built from thoughts of fear. Depression is built from thoughts of failure. To avoid anxiety and panic, avoid thoughts that taste of fear. To avoid depression, avoid thoughts that taste of failure or hopelessness.

Anger, resentment, frustration all have their taste as do thoughts of kindness, generosity, and love. Just as negative content tastes of pain, *the taste of truth is joy*. Stay with contemplations that taste of joy, which we will detail in the next chapter. Steer the mind there.

You live in the climate of your psyche, the most intimate aspect of your experience. You create the climate of your psyche, pleasant or unpleasant, with each thought you think. You can create a climate of peace and kindness, or a climate of anger and resentment depending on how you behave internally.

Certain outer behaviors are healthy and others are not. It is wise to avoid unhealthy behavior or you might land in jail! But thought is *a subtle form of behavior. Thought is inner behavior.* And just as it is wise to behave well outwardly, it wise to behave well inwardly, to make good thought-choices. Just as you would not rob a bank, it is wise to avoid mental behavior that crosses a certain line. Why? Because *every thought you think you do to yourself.* You are the immediate and direct recipient of each thought you think, for better or worse.

Don't worry if thoughts simply pop into mind. That is to be expected. If thoughts are disregarded without involvement they make no impact. There is only impact when thoughts are entertained; then thinking becomes inner behavior that has its consequences.

With anger, for example, it may seem as if you are focused outwardly on the object of your anger - that good for nothing husband of yours, what a bum he is. But as you think angrily about the bum, you acquiesce to anger in your own psyche. You choose to act angrily - internally. With each angry thought, you affect the climate of your psyche, you poison your own well. *Every thought you think you do to yourself.* You are the immediate recipient of your thought-choices and immediately feel their emotional impact. It is your blood that boils and your mind that reels. Never mind about the bum.

While complaining, it may seem as if you are focused on the object of complaint, but you are the perpetrator of complaining; the climate of your psyche becomes one of complaint. So it was said, "Do not worry about the splinter in your neighbor's eye, concern yourself with the beam in your own eye." In what negativity do you indulge? Notice your transgressions and focus less on the sins of others.

It works both ways, of course. With each loving thought, your mind tastes happiness. Each generous thought is a gift to yourself and to the world.

I have heard the argument made that there is merit to negative thinking. In a sense, yes. If your thought is, "Don't expect very much," but voiced in a tone of compassion as if to say, "Don't set yourself up for disappointment, things may just not work out," then the tone of the thought is actually kind and its impact will be kindness. If the thought is voiced in a tone of bitterness as if to say, "Nothing has ever gone right and nothing *will* ever go right," then bitterness will be the impact of the thought. The issue is not so much *what* is said but *how* it is said, the tone of the thought, its taste. We will return to this shortly.

The cause of suffering, then, is a misuse of mind in either process or content. Obsessing - the wayward mind, the mind out of control, relentless thinking regardless of its content (even Cheerios) - is painful. Obsessing with thoughts that are negative in content is worse. Each negative thought is a self inflicted pain; persisting in these thoughts will result in pronounced symptoms of distress.

Your mind is a stew. You are the chef. Each thought is an ingredient that contributes to the overall flavor of the stew; one that is delicious with love, kindness and generosity, or one that tastes otherwise.

Placebo

He had become accustomed to using medication for relaxation and sleep, and wondered whether he would be able to sleep without medication.

As an experiment, I suggested to him, let's try using the placebo effect. If you are given a pill and believe it will induce relaxation, you will tend to relax even if the pill is only a placebo. Let's go one step further and *imagine* that you are being given a beneficial pill. I don't have a pill to give you, but let's imagine I did, that you have been given a new relaxation medication that is getting rave reviews in all the media. It is a biochemical sensation. As soon as it is taken, deep and blissful relaxation spreads throughout the body like warm honey. Your limbs relax and hang without encumbrance from the frame. The muscles release all tension. The skin covering the muscles settles with the pull of gravity. All worries are forgotten, all thoughts of past and future disappear, and the mind slowly sinks into an ever deepening state of peace. Like water seeping into cloth, a blissful peace seeps into the mind and body and spreads until every last corner is saturated. Imagine the relaxation produced by this wonder drug and see if mind alone can create the same effect.

The Taste of Thought

I was talking with a man who hates his job. He feels enormous resentment toward his employer, a public institution. The institution terminated the position he labored at for many years. He was directed to apply for a newly created position and was lucky to secure that position, keeping his seniority and benefits. But the sacrifices he made, virtually giving his life to his work - the late nights away from his family, the times he drove to work in a blizzard - all this was overlooked and unappreciated. The institution was content hanging him out to dry. He derived no pleasure from work; it was a sacrifice he made for the benefit of his family, his precious children and baby granddaughter. He lived for them, his only source of joy.

Let's try an experiment. Think of your granddaughter. Say her name to yourself inwardly. I see a smile of pure love come to your face. Now think of your employer. Wow, your expression has turned into a scowl! Again think of your baby grandchild; the smile returns. Now think of your boss. Scowl.

Each thought carries its association. Each thought has its taste. Choose your contemplation wisely. Let mind work for rather than against your purposes.

Potato Chips

I like potato chips more than I ought to. I stopped in the supermarket one evening on my way home from work, did the usual food shopping, but broke down and bought a seemingly harmless bag of chips. It was the end of the day, I was hungry, and I parked the bag of chips on the front seat of the car as I drove. By the time I got home, I had eaten half the bag! I felt terrible, had no dinner that night, the chips effectively were my dinner. Yuck.

There are wholesome thoughts and unwholesome thoughts, wholesome contemplations and unwholesome contemplations. You are always focused in one way or another. Consume lots of unwholesome thoughts, half a bag worth, and you will make yourself sick. Consume lots of fear and you are sure to become panicky. Consume lots of failure and you are sure to give up hope. Bad tasting thoughts are like eating chips for dinner; you will become ill. The first step to feeling well is to stop indulging in the junk food of the mind.

Habits

Water flows down from the mountains in clear, rushing streams along the ancient riverbed, carved through the rock over time. Ways of thinking are carved in the brain like water which flows through the riverbed.

The water flows through its well-worn pathways. Mental pathways are similarly carved in the brain, in the mind and, unless consciously redirected, thoughts will tend to flow along the path of the familiar.

You will tend to regard and react to life in habitual ways like water which flows through the riverbed. It takes conscious attention to divert attention from the familiar path.

In other words, the mind has habits - and some bad habits. Like any bad habit - since thought is behavior - the habit needs to be broken. If I bite my fingernails, for example, I need to break the habit. Each time I notice that my fingers have unconsciously drifted into my mouth, I withdraw them. If I think badly, I similarly need to drop the bad behavior when I notice that I have drifted there and redirect in healthier ways.

Hypnosis

There are two stages to the practice of hypnosis: induction and suggestion. The induction is the inducing of relaxation, preparing the mind for the suggestions to follow. In the classic image of induction, the hypnotist waves a pocket watch and says, "You are getting very sleepy." Once the subject is relaxed and receptive, once the induction is in place, suggestions are made to influence the mind. The suggestions "take" because the mind is ready. Induction is preparing the soil; suggestion is planting the seed.

Essentially, in the receptive state, the hypnotic subject "agrees" to the suggestions made by the hypnotist. She "signs on" to the suggestion. Nisargadatta uses the example of a package being delivered; you take delivery or can refuse to take delivery of the package. So if the hypnotist suggests, "Imagine you are lying on a tropical beach at sunset. You hear the waves lapping at the shore. The sun warms your body and you feel very peaceful," the subject inwardly says, "Okay, I'll go along." That is the hallmark of a good hypnotic subject: one who is willing to surrender to suggestion.

When I was in graduate school, I took a course in hypnosis at Massachusetts General Hospital. During the course a film was shown. The film was of a woman receiving a Cesarean section with no or very little anesthesia (I don't remember exactly). The woman was an unusually good hypnotic subject which means she was unusually able to surrender to hypnotic suggestions. During the procedure she was lying prone, the hypnotist sat on a stool by her ear and whispered something like, "You are in a forest near a babbling brook. You hear the music of the brook and are enchanted. Dappled light paints the forest floor. You are so grateful to be sitting in this shaded forest with the brook singing nearby." And the woman responded dreamily, "Yes, it is so peaceful here, how beautiful the shade and sound of the water." Meanwhile, she was being cut with a scalpel.

The woman had signed on, she bought into the suggestions that were being offered. She was immersed in a process of guided imagery, so much so that she lost herself in images of beauty and hardly noticed the pain. Was she in a forest listening to a babbling brook? Of course not; she was in surgery. But she so invested herself in the images that a beautiful forest was her experienced reality.

Whatever thought you take seriously becomes your experienced reality, not necessarily because it is true, but only because you believe it.

This is a very important principle. Just yesterday, Julie, a very charming young woman told me, "I feel like I'm the least interesting person on the planet." If she believes this negative thought, it will be her experienced reality and she will become ill. I want to say, like Cher in Moonstruck, "Julie, snap out of it!" Consider instead that you are God.

Children are especially programmable. No induction is necessary as the child is in a natural state of receptivity and suggestions take spontaneously. The child is effectively hypnotized by the suggestions he encounters in early life, and these suggestions contribute to the child's identity.

If the child is not treated tenderly, he may conclude that he is not that worthy, not good enough. While not at all true, this may nevertheless become a longstanding belief based on the suggestions received when the mind was impressionable. The child's mind is as if hypnotized or programmed, and these programs form the basis for self image and world view that often have to be un-hypnotized or un-programmed in the adult work of conscious growth.

There are two approaches to negative programming. The mind can be *re*-programmed with positive suggestions in the process of Positive-thinking. Or the mind can be *un*-programmed in No-thinking.

Chicken Thoughts

Julie could never win her mother's approval. Whatever she did somehow was not good enough. Even as an adult, Julie's children were never dressed properly in her mother's eyes, nor was the town she lived in up to her mother's standards. Julie seemingly could do nothing right.

"Have you heard the saying: parents push your buttons so well because they installed the buttons in the first place? Julie, your mother is pushing your buttons but her behavior is not really the problem; besides you may never gain her approval. The problem is that you have not dismantled the buttons she installed so long ago, which are now perpetuated by your own thought process.

Imagine that someone volunteers to go onstage during a performance by a hypnotist. The subject is hypnotized into believing that he is a chicken. In a relaxed state, once the induction is in place, the hypnotist makes the suggestion that the subject is actually a chicken. The subject accepts. He effectively says, 'OK, I'll go along,' and so buys into the chicken thought. He starts to cluck and flap his wings like a chicken, it is all very amusing. Then the hypnotist says, 'When I snap my fingers you will realize that you are no longer a chicken.' The subject then lets go of, he disinvests from the chicken thought, and stops clucking and flapping. He bought into and acted out the suggestion until he was disaffected of the belief that he was a chicken, the hypnosis wore off, and he returned to his normal self; everyday hypnosis.

Your mother has you hypnotized into believing that you do nothing right and that you need her approval. She pushes those buttons and you cluck and flap, but only because you still accept the suggestion, only because the programming remains intact. The thought that you need her approval, just like the thought that you are a chicken, has no reality whatsoever but seems real as long as you believe it. You must disaffect yourself of this programming.

Every time your mother gives you the message that you are failing, every time she pushes that button - stimulus and response - observe your programmed response and reject the thought that you are failing. The thought will come up from time to time because it has momentum, and your mother may try to activate the programming. But if you observe your programmed response without buying into the thought that you need your mother's approval, you will become free from the hypnosis.

The operative factor is awareness. Become aware of rather than embedded in the programming and the programming will wear off from lack of sustenance."

Stories

As you carry on the conversation with yourself, you are telling yourself stories, one chicken thought after another. You visit and revisit the different story lines that make up your overall life story: story lines about the relationships in your life; the grievances in your life; the desires in your life, what you want, what you don't want (craving, obsessing). The stories are sometimes very compelling and sometimes wearisome. The stories create the contours of the ego, the one speaking in his or her own voice. However, the stories are entirely illusory, as real as a mirage.

Why? *Because thoughts are not real. (And if thoughts are not real, then the mind, which is the activity of thinking, is also not real)!* Thoughts are empty vapor that have no real substance. Thoughts seem real only when and because they are taken as real. If I take a thought seriously, like the thought that I am a chicken, I turn an empty thought into a belief that shapes the ego and the belief seems real and significant. If I did not take the thought seriously, it would disappear without consequence. If I sustain the thought by taking it seriously, I have given credence to an illusion that becomes my reality only because I have made it my reality. I create an illusion and then am lost in the illusion of my own making.

Thoughts are about the remembered past or imagined future. Thoughts are about *the elsewhere*, something other than the immediacy of here and now. As you read these pages, if your mind wanders it wanders into *the elsewhere*. When the mind is quiet and without thought, there is only the immediacy of here and now and dilemma disappears.

Sailor Bob Adamson, a spiritual teacher, wrote a book entitled, "What's Wrong With Right Now - Unless You Think About It." Great title, reminiscent of Hamlet saying, "Nothing either good or bad but thinking makes it so." Sailor Bob's title expresses a very important concept. This and every moment is perfectly satisfactory *until you start thinking*, until craving judges this moment as unsatisfactory for whatever reason. If your mind stopped, if you stopped thinking, you would return to the peace inherent in the simplicity of Being.

Each thought taps you on the shoulder and invites you to participate in its drama. You then have the opportunity to accept the invitation or not. I was speaking in session with Rebecca who has anxiety. She blurted out, "What if I'm untreatable?" I started to laugh. How clever she was in creating anxiety, how clever fear in sustaining itself. The thought was a masterpiece of anxiety. Of course, the thought is terrifying if taken seriously; fear will have done its job successfully.

Let's say she takes the thought seriously, buys into it. In doing so, she gives energy to a story which becomes her reality only because she has made it so. She could reject the thought but was not careful enough to do so in this case. The thought is equivalent to the story title, "What if I'm Untreatable." She now has the opportunity to further develop the story. The next sentence, she said, the next line in the script would be, "Well, then I'll end up in a padded room." What a scriptwriter she is, surely destined for Hollywood! The next line would be, "Then I will lose my job and family, my daughter will have to visit me in an institution," and on it goes.

If she pays attention, she will notice that these thoughts taste of fear and unhappiness. The initial thought, "What if I'm untreatable," already tastes like panic. If she persists, her psyche will become more and more tainted with fear. If she notices the thought without involvement, it disappears without consequence; the thought has no inherent reality.

Stories are most apparent when someone is delusional. Say I believe that I have landed from Mars. I believe that I am a native of Mars here for just a little sojourn, while my family is back on Mars waiting. You might look at me and say, "Solomon, you are not from Mars. You were born in New York. Snap out of it!" But if I hold onto the thought, if I really buy into it, as far as I'm concerned I'm from Mars. Mars is my reality because I have made it so.

What is your story? Commonly told, unhappy stories are "I'm not good enough, I doubt myself, I need her to love me, I need approval from others, I need to have a perfect body." These thoughts are about as real as the thought that I am a chicken. However, if taken seriously these thoughts - and the thought that I am a chicken - can seem entirely real, and become experienced reality.

My professor in college used to say that philosophy is the questioning of presuppositions. There is another level of story altogether. What beliefs, what presuppositions have you not questioned? Apart from the everyday dramas, are there deeper stories that you accept as real? My religion is the truest and the best? God is far away in heaven after I die? I am this body? *I was born?*

Story or Fact?

"I am" alone is; and not "I am so and so," or "I am such and such." When existence is absolute, it is right; when it is particularized, it is wrong. That is the whole truth. (Talks with Ramana Maharshi. P. 275).

I remember speaking with a woman who said, "I really am not good enough. Why is that not just a true statement, a statement of fact?"

The following discussion is a bit premature so bear with me; this will be elaborated in the chapter on No-thinking. But the short answer is: *all thoughts pertaining to the personal self are stories, chicken thoughts.* Like a mirage the personal self, the ego is itself not real. As Krishnamurti stated, "The thinker is the thought... there is no thinker separate from thought." The thinker, the ego, arises with and is part-and-parcel of the thought spoken in the ego's own voice. But the ego is just an impression, like a collage, a composite image composed of many other images, each of which is unreal. "I'm not good enough," is one such image that contributes to the overall collage of the ego. (This is the Buddhist tenet of no-self; the ego does not really exist, it is an illusion).

Let's say I am wandering in the desert, terribly thirsty. I see a pool of water in the distance amid the sands. I walk quickly to reach the refreshing water but, as I approach, on closer investigation I realize that I made a mistake. I misperceived. The water never existed.

The personal self, the ego, like the mirage, appears to be real but on closer investigation is seen to be unreal. If you examine all thoughts that pertain to the ego, of which the collage of the ego is composed - like the thought "I'm not good enough" - you will discover upon investigation that the thoughts flee like ants from under a suddenly lifted rock.

Try it. Look at thoughts carefully. Wait for a thought to appear. When looking directly at a thought, if there is no involvement, the thought vanishes. What remains is the looking: Consciousness, Being - *You* - the context within which the thought arose and which persists with or without, before and after the thought. (See Talking or Listening in the chapter on No-Thinking for further discussion).

The sense of Being prior to thought is the Self. The statement "I'm not good enough" is an idea that may seem real, and which may gather momentum through a lack of clarity. But when I look more clearly I see that I made a mistake, I took myself to be something that I am not.

Ramana Maharshi has said: "'I am' is the reality. I am this or that is unreal. 'I am' is truth, another name for the Self." (Godman, David. Be As You Are. P. 43). In other words, your true reality is "I am." To say anything more - I am this or that - I'm not good enough - is to entertain unreality.

"'I am' is truth, another name for the Self." *You* most certainly are. The fact of your Being is inescapable, the context within which thoughts and all experience arise. But when you say, "I'm not good enough" then, like a teenager getting mixed up with the wrong crowd, your true Self has become associated with a bad influence and needs to straighten itself out.

When you say "I'm not good enough," what does "I," the subject, refer to before it is modified by the predicate "not good enough"?

The mirage is dissipated when the subject - "I" - extricates itself from everything with which it has wrongly identified. The "I" shakes off the dust - the misperception, the case of mistaken identity, the illusion, the stories. You approach your purity free from all entanglements. You can then look at another and see their purity as well, beyond all the stories in which they too have become entangled.

The collage of thoughts and images creates the sense of an ego. The ego is not an entity but *patterns of thinking*. (I will often say to patients, "There is no such thing as poor self-esteem, there are only patterns of thought"). The mind in its proper place is silent and peaceful like water without any wind. Any thought is a gust on the surface of silence. From the perspective of silence, all thought is an anomaly that appears from and disappears back into the silence from which it emerged. Thus, any modification pertaining to the "I" is thought vapor which, if not sustained, disappears without merit. "I'm not good enough," is about as real as the thought, "I am a chicken." From the perspective of the mind still and clear, I can't take either thought seriously.

The What and the How

The Self is beyond any modification, subject without predicate. However, it is always possible to make relative statements such as, "I am a psychologist." Sure, on one level I am a psychologist, that is a role I play, but the role is not a reflection of who I truly am.

It is also possible to make rational statements about a state of affairs. For example, Rebecca wondered, "What if I'm untreatable?"

In her case, the statement was made in a tone of panic; fear was making up stories. One must become savvy to the tricks of fear and mind in general. Rebecca has learnt to do this, she no longer torments herself with panic thoughts, and anxiety has become less of an issue.

But let's say that someone does have an illness that is deemed untreatable. In that case, "What if I'm untreatable?" is a reasonable conjecture. The salient point is *how* is the question asked not *what* is being asked. Is the question being asked rationally or irrationally? The tone, the taste of the thought provides the answer.

So there is a discernment to be made. "What if I'm untreatable?" can be a reasonable conjecture if spoken rationally and the tone of the thought will reflect this. It can also be the voice of fear if spoken irrationally and in a panic. A discernment needs to be made, the impact of the thought on the climate of the psyche. This can be hard to express in writing but is obvious from the different tones with which a statement can be inflected.

A quiet mind is able to perceive clearly and to make these discernments. I may rationally discern that an illness is untreatable and consider what course of action needs to be taken, rather than irrationally and unnecessarily frightening myself. I can discern that a political course is unwise, that someone is depressed and why, that a salesman is asking too much money for a car. I clearly see what is in front of me and respond appropriately. If I see a bus coming quickly towards me, I get out of the road. If the sky is cloudy, I grab my umbrella.

Let's go back to the employee with the mean boss. Sometimes his boss is mean, absolutely. That is an accurate perception. When that is so, as with the approaching bus, he should respond appropriately to the occasion and... next moment.

You live in the climate of your psyche. My boss being mean does not need to have *any* impact on my psyche which ideally remains balanced, kind, expressing its naturally peaceful state. My boss's meanness is an expression of *his* psyche. At my best, I do not react to meanness because my upset button has been dismantled and there is no reactivity left to be pushed. I am firmly established in peace. To react with indignation indicates that I still have an indignation button. This is a reflection of *my* state of mind.

At my best, I respond to my boss's insensitive behavior with compassion because I sense the pain that is being expressed in his meanness. I am also able to see beyond the meanness to his purity. I remain the presence of love which is best for myself, for my boss, and for the world. From this state of mind, it is easy to turn the other cheek.

I would suggest that every adult take absolute responsibility for the climate of his or her psyche. Do not blame anyone or anything for your inner state. If you are upset, don't blame your boss. From a wide range of possible responses you chose upset; you could have chosen compassion. Upset is present because an upset thought arose, was invested in, and so made real.

Your boss is one of life's fingers pushing your buttons. The reactive mind is yours; thank your boss for showing you this corner in your psyche where ignorance hides. This is what Ram Dass means when he says that, "Suffering is grace." Suffering shows where buttons remain to be dismantled so that a deeper freedom can be realized.

I knew a man who often argued with his adult son. Eventually, the son grew tired of arguing and distanced himself from his father. The father complained, "But he was disrespectful. How would you react if your child treated you with disrespect?"

"I would probably say, 'Is something bothering you, sweetheart?' I would not say, 'How dare you talk to me in that manner. You're grounded!'" Your response to disrespect remains an expression of your state of Being. Try to remain the presence of love. This is easiest when you remain as your Self because its nature - your nature - *is* love, the state of the heart.

But there is one nuance to be added. Even while centered in the heart, the entire palette of emotions and responses remains available. I may express myself forcefully at times, as appropriate, as an expression of wisdom, not insanity. From a position of balance, I may discern that a forceful response is best in a given situation and, like a composer, choose force from my tonal palette as the most appropriate and even compassionate response to the situation at hand, taking all things into consideration.

Love is not different from the Self. Love of an object is of an inferior order and cannot endure, whereas the Self *is* Love; in other words, God is Love. (Talks with Ramana Maharshi. P. 328).

Untreatable

A universe that frustrates the very desires it ordains.

The crucifixion as metaphor:
can you maintain perfect peace, the heart,
even while being externally seared?
That is the test.
Thus does life offer adversity, trials, crucifixions great and small,
to test and strengthen inner equilibrium.
Can you then, while on the cross, under the pressure of adversity,
transcend reactivity - fear, doubt - why have you forsaken me? -
and remain still, aligned with perfect peace,
the underlying depth prior to the arising of the reactive mind?

The Only Thing That Can Hurt You

I see a patient with social anxiety; he is nervous around people. When in public, he fears that others are scrutinizing him and adversely judging his appearance and behavior. He becomes very self conscious and eventually needs to retreat from the public realm.

I say to him and to almost everyone: "You do not need to worry about what goes on in someone else's head. You are only affected by what goes on in *your* head. Short of being physically attacked, the only thing that hurts you are your thoughts, not anyone else's. The fear of scrutiny is a thought that arises in your mind; you then taste self generated fear. Even if you are being scrutinized and judged, if you remain balanced and your fear reaction is not triggered, the thoughts of others will have no impact."

What hurts me are only the thoughts I entertain in my own head. If I am being unfairly criticized, screamed at no less, but feel compassionate toward the one doing the screaming, my experience is compassion not rebuke. If I am being blamed but am compassionate toward my accuser, my experience remains compassion. If in my mind the thought arises, "I am such a loser," or "*He* is such a loser," and I accept that thought, the climate of my psyche is affected, but not by the blame being hurled in my direction, which only reflects the psyche of the one doing the hurling.

The archetypal example of this is Jesus on the cross who says, "Forgive them for they know not what they do." Even while being tortured, he retains a mind state of compassion toward his torturers.

A modern day representative is the Dalai Lama. While his Tibetan culture and people are decimated by the Chinese, he holds to the practice of compassion which alone, he says, can transform human brutality in the long run. Now, the best response toward Chinese aggression is debatable and people of wisdom can legitimately differ as to how the situation should be handled. But the response is best pursued from a balanced mind or a cycle of negativity will result.

Whatever your mood, you are creating that mood with your thoughts. To love unconditionally is to be, like Superman, invulnerable.

Abuse

Taryn is in love with Joseph and is planning to merge her life with his. She plans to leave the United States and move overseas to join him. But even while she is making arrangements to leave, Joseph is being surprisingly mean on the phone - if he even returns her calls. She is starting to wonder whether he is abusive, and why does she tolerate the abuse anyway? In her mind she has angry conversations with Joseph, telling him off. "Just come clean, why don't you? If you don't want me there, just say so!" She thinks about him constantly; she can't stop thinking. She doesn't sleep well, her heart is starting to race, and her hands to tremble.

Remember that symptoms are the grooves on the side of the highway that rumble your tires and awaken you to the fact that you are veering off course. The symptom is your friend; the organism giving you valuable feedback. Straighten the wheel before veering even farther off course, before the imbalance causing the symptom becomes worse.

Taryn, I said, Joseph is certainly pushing your buttons. I agree, your agitation does not come out of nowhere, there is a trigger: Joseph's insensitivity. But within you is the capacity to obsess. If there were no such capacity you would see the situation clearly and respond appropriately. You might still decide to make the trip or call the trip off, as you wish. In any case, obsessing needs to be controlled, a bad use of mind.

There are two doomed love affairs here: the love affair with an abusive man, and the love affair with an abusive mind.

Flash Quiz: Do the Math

Let's review. You are talking to yourself in your mind. Your mind *is* this talking to yourself. You are talking to yourself about the situations in your life and your place among those situations. This is storytelling, obsessing about your dilemma. All this talking, all these stories revolve around and create the impression of an ego, a personal self, the one who is doing the talking in his or her own voice, and to whom all the stories relate. All the stories are about what has already happened and what might happen in the future, not what is actually present because this moment is immediate and prior to story.

Let's do the math.

Thinking = Mind = Ego = Personal Self = Stories =
Past and Future = Dilemma = Suffering.

These terms are all synonymous. Thinking is mind and mind is ego. The mind/ego is also the personal self. The mind/ego/personal self is built out of stories of past and future and it has a problem.

How to solve the problem inherent in the mind/ego/personal self? Lose the personal self to find the greater Self. The personal self must die so that the greater Self is as if reborn.

Sun Behind Clouds

A common metaphor for the spiritual process is the sun emerging from behind the clouds. The sun is always in the sky but sometimes it is obscured by clouds. On cloudy days, if you had just landed from

Mars (as I have), you wouldn't even know there was a sun. There is little light and little warmth. However, as the clouds disperse, the sun peeks through here and there. Some light and warmth bathe the earth. When the clouds dissolve completely, the sun is radiantly apparent.

As you progress spiritually, the clouds of mind disperse and rays of sun and light, warmth and happiness peek through. As the clouds disperse, as mind becomes quieter, more and more a non-issue, wellness begins to shine. The wellness, like the sun, was always present, our innate nature, but was obscured for a while by clouds of confusion, the density of mind.

Meditation 101

To make the concept of thought-as-story clearer, let's introduce a basic notion of meditation. A universal meditation technique is meditation on breathing. The simplified instructions for one form of breathing meditation are as follows. Focus your attention on your breathing. Listen to the breathing as if you were listening to the waves at the ocean. The breath mirrors the cosmic movement of rise and fall. For example, each month the moon starts as a new moon, perfectly empty, it waxes and grows more full each night until it reaches perfect fullness. Once perfectly full the moon begins to wane, to empty, until it returns to the state of perfect emptiness, and the cycle renews. Similarly your lungs, like the new moon, begin each breath cycle empty, they fill until reaching perfect fullness, and then the lungs empty. Each day the tides rise until reaching maximum fullness, and then the tides fall. Each year, as if the earth breathes in, the days grow long and then, as if the earth breathes out, the days grow short. Each breath cycle is a movement of birth and death, the underlying organic rhythm. So listen to your breath as if you were listening to waves at the ocean which also rise and fall. The breath provides a convenient focus because it is always available, and focusing on the breath has the effect of calming mind and body. If attention drifts from breathing and the mind wanders, when this is recognized simply, neutrally, say "thinking, thinking," to yourself, as a way of acknowledging that thinking has occurred and bring attention back to breathing.

What this technique does is nullify the entire thought process. By labeling the wandering mind as "thinking, thinking," and coming back to the primary focus on breathing, the entire content of thinking is made irrelevant. It is mere "thinking, thinking," a wandering mind, nothing more. We notice the process - that thinking has taken place - without any involvement in the content. With one fell swoop the charge is neutralized, the significance removed from all thought content. The plug is pulled on the enterprise of story making.

It is like saying, "Oh, I've wandered into the 'My boss is a bum' story. I've wandered into 'I'm not good enough.' I am back in 'What if I'm untreatable.' Not interested. Can't be bothered. Mere thinking, thinking. Back to breathing." By withdrawing involvement, by no longer juicing the story and so making it real, the story has become meaningless, mere mental noise. The thought dies on the vine, never having ripened.

Thinking is talking to yourself inwardly. If you do not enter the conversation, the conversation ends like a bad date. A thought appears and bursts like a bubble if it is not sustained. For the conversation to continue, you must enter the conversation and think it along. Without doing so, all stories disappear without significance. You come to understand, if you do not lend reality to thoughts, that no thoughts are real.

Movie Projector

You are built like a movie projector. The heart of the projector is the light. The light is Innately Creative and so animates whatever film is placed before it. The film may be a happy story or a sad story. The light does not care; it imparts reality impartially, lending apparent reality to any image. The images which the light illuminates are the images held in mind, which create the mood of experienced reality.

In this metaphor, the heart is represented by the light and the deviation from the heart into mind is represented by the images which the light animates. Mind can move in many ways. The images in mind can be destructive or constructive. Destructive images result in Negative-thinking; constructive images result in Positive-thinking which we will discuss in detail in the next chapter.

Your essential nature is light, pure Being, Innate Creativity. The name of the light is "I Am" or simply "I." In other words, the light at the heart of Being - pure "I Am-ness" - precedes all the images in mind which are secondary modifications of the light. "I," the light of Being, is pre-story, pre-drama, subject without predicate. It is the source from which thought and story arise. Being is always present, always operative, but to apprehend the nature of Being - your essential nature - more clearly you must awaken from hypnosis, the dream of being an ego. You must drop all thought, which is a deviation from the heart, and return to the heart itself.

The Innately Creative light of Being imparts reality to any image through which it shines. Your mind and its thoughts are the images. The thought may be, "I'm not good enough, I doubt myself, I am a loser," or "I am capable of great success," sad stories, happy stories. The root of all the stories is "I." All the stories emerge from and have their source in "I." The "I," the creative light, is modified through the images held in mind.

The images are not fundamentally real in the sense that thoughts are not real. The deeper reality on which all the images depend is the light. But if you are going to animate an image, it might as well be a good one.

Pure Being, the light itself, the "I" prior to any story, is the peace of No-thinking. It is the peace of undisturbed Consciousness; still water; the heart. Because there is no movement and inherent peace, there is an *absence of desire*. Desire is a movement away from stillness. Desire is a stirring of mind which is absent in pure Being.

However, within the world of Becoming, happy stories are better than unhappy stories. By changing the image held in mind from a painful to a joyful image, the mood and to some extent actual experience will also change. If you are unhappy, mind must be awry in process and content. The mind is either too busy or focused on images of lack. Change the image held before the light to an image of beauty, and mood will also change. Positive-thinking is focused on attaining *the fulfillment of desire,* on making the content of life more beautiful, more to your liking.

Positive-thinking, focused on *the fulfillment of desire*, is about having a happy, rewarding dream rather than a nightmare. No-thinking, *the absence of desire*, is about waking up from dreaming.

Failure

Jason is convinced he will fail. In effect, he meditates on failure. Jason has been successfully hypnotized into believing a story of failure, poor self worth, and takes it as true. He does not see that failure is simply an image in mind that only has as much reality as he imparts, a chicken thought. It is real because he believes it is real. But another story could be equally true.

Jason compensates for his assumption of failure by pleasuring himself in addictive ways. He overeats and drinks too much alcohol. There has to be pleasure *somewhere* in life! Jason experiences both depression and anxiety. Depression because he is convinced he will fail and anxiety because, since disaster is inevitable, the world and the future are scary.

Jason, of course, is fundamentally the creative light and is using his Innate Creativity to give reality to the images of fear and failure he holds in mind, on which he unknowingly meditates. His fundamental nature of "I Am," the subject, is attaching itself to the predicate

"A Failure," and so the title of his story is "I Am a Failure," a story of unhappiness.

Jason needs to change his mind. If he is going to meditate on some image it might as well be an image of beauty. If he is going to animate a story, why not animate a story entitled, "Success!"

The Mechanics of Suffering

Before leaving Negative-thinking let's review the mechanics of suffering.

Let's say a child fears that there is a boogie man in his room. While the child believes the thought that there is a boogie man, he is frightened, he must sleep with the light on, and leave the door to the closet open. Can the boogie man be removed from the room? Of course not, there is no boogie man, it is just imagination, just a thought in mind. As soon as the thought of the boogie man is released, the boogie man and the problem disappear.

Let's go back to the person hypnotized on stage. The person is told that he is a chicken. Under hypnosis, he accepts the thought that he is a chicken and clucks and flaps his wings. Is he a chicken? Of course not. But as long as he accepts that thought, chicken is his reality. When the hypnotist snaps his finger and says, "You are no longer a chicken," the subject releases the thought and the chicken disappears. He was never a chicken but bought into that reality for a while.

The starring roles in the mechanics of suffering are played by fear and doubt. Fear, especially in the form of worry, is very prevalent. Fear and worry are always about the future, what awful thing might happen down the road. Spend enough time with worry and you will certainly become ill. Doubt, especially in the form of the "I'm not good enough" thought, is also quite prevalent. Neither of these thoughts are real; they are real to the extent that they are invested in. Signing onto negative thought drives the mechanics of suffering.

What is real? The Real-Maker not the image made apparently real. The light in the projector is real and lends apparent reality to the image held before it. "I" am real. I may then make the boogie man thought appear real, or the chicken thought appear real, or fear and doubt appear real, but they are all unreal images held before the real light of awareness. *You* are real, not your stories. As soon as the stories are relinquished, they disappear. But if you are going to animate a story, it might as well be a good one, success rather than failure.

There is really good news in this. Suffering is transitory. Suffering is the result of a misunderstanding, a bad use of mind. Your nature is inevitably light. Release the boogie man thought, the chicken thought, the fear and doubt, and happiness is your nature and destiny.

If You Can Work Yourself Up, You Can Work Yourself Down

A rubber band resting on a table is in a state of zero stress. (Here the zero stress state is the heart). If the rubber band is stretched it deviates from the zero stress state, the rubber band becomes tense, tight; stress has entered the rubber band. The more it is stretched, the tighter it becomes. But stress is not the natural condition of the rubber band. The natural condition of the rubber band is while resting on the table in the zero stress state.

Similarly, when you blow up a balloon tension accumulates in the balloon. The more air, the more tension. If the balloon is very full, a slight poke can bring about an intense reaction: the balloon might explode. The balloon, when very full, is in a high stress state and slight pressure produces disproportionate reactions. But if air and tension are let out of the balloon, it becomes less reactive. Pressure from outside will have no impact, as there is plenty of room to absorb the external pressure.

The rubber band and the balloon represent the organism in a state of stress: worked up. When the organism is worked up, tight and contracted, symptoms arise that signify a deviation from the natural, zero stress state. Discomfort is felt in body and mind. But the organism does not want to stay worked up. The muscles do not want to stay knotted or in a state of spasm. If given the opportunity, the organism will gradually relax, the knots will unwind, and the zero stress state will be restored. Healing practices like meditation allow the organism the opportunity to release constriction and return to zero stress. If you can work yourself up then, by withdrawing from maladaptive behaviors that generate stress, by allowing the body to heal, you can work yourself down.

Warm and Cold

As a child, I played the game of warm and cold. I would hide something, my friend would look for the object, and I would say, "You're getting warmer," as he got close, "You're getting colder," as he went in the wrong direction.

Peace works in much the same way. Peace is biofeedback from the organism that you are getting warmer, moving in the right direction, toward the heart. Its absence, misery, is biofeedback that you are going astray and need to change course.

It is not unusual to persist in well intentioned but misleading ideas about peace, spirituality, or enlightenment. We have conceptions as to what these might look like, and where they might be found. But it may be simpler to follow the biofeedback from the organism, moving in the direction of the greater warmth, peace, and love, forgetting conceptions altogether.

I know a woman who was delusional and believed that she was toxic to others. Her good intention was to protect others from exposure to her toxicity. While her intention to do no harm was admirable, as she persisted in paranoia and went to greater pains to avoid the harm she might cause, her isolation and suffering grew as well.

I tried to play the warm-cold game with her. Could she put her thoughts and beliefs aside and orient herself using biofeedback from the organism? Could she sense whether following her beliefs brought about the warmth of peace, or the cold of isolation? (This reminds me of pilots who are taught, in bad weather, to navigate by feedback from their gauges rather than by visual cues which may offer distorted information. Use feedback from one set of gauges and not from another set, which might mislead). I asked if she could *feel* whether she was getting warmer or colder, more or less peaceful, and move in the direction of warmth, using the biofeedback from her organism as guidance, rather than her well intentioned but misguided beliefs.

Flash Quiz: Equations

worked up = colder = mind

Worked down = Warmer = Heart

CHAPTER III:

POSITIVE-THINKING

Grabbing the Reins

The first step in the psychological/spiritual journey is the realization that the galloping horse of mind actually has reins. Maybe you hadn't noticed the reins previously but you do now. Without reins you were at the mercy of the galloping, but that no longer needs to be so. Yes, there are reins, you can grab them and get the galloping under control, maybe even bring it to a halt. The mind, its pace, its movement, its *process*, and the thoughts and images it contains, its *content*, do not have to be taken as given.

The idea of reins is important. Evolutionary forward progress is a movement from unconsciousness to Consciousness. The galloping mind is a primitive unconscious state, a mind in motion but almost at random, conditioning just playing itself out. Holding onto the reins implies applying conscious control to a movement that was running wild. Harnessing the movement stops its destructiveness and turns it constructive. The unrestrained mind causes suffering for self and world. The conscious mind yields peace.

Positive-thinking exercises control over the mind so that mind becomes friendlier, more adaptive, working for rather than against your purposes. Positive-thinking operates entirely within the domain of mind; mind acts upon itself to become more hospitable. In Positive-thinking the mind consciously focuses on images of beauty and abundance which bear the taste of happiness. As such, Positive-thinking is primarily focused on changing the *content* of thought. The *process* of thought, the very activity of mind, will be addressed more specifically in No-thinking where the objective is the withdrawal from all movement.

Speaking broadly, Positive-thinking is the domain of (Western) psychology and No-thinking is the domain of (Eastern) spirituality. Western psychology is about improving the mind, making the mind a more comfortable climate in which to live. The aim of psychology, as commonly practiced, is to change for the better the images held before the light of awareness. The Western focus is on *the fulfillment of desire,* mind at the service of creating beautiful experiences in thought and in life. Eastern psychology or higher spirituality, on the other hand, aspires to the domain of No–thinking, silence, going *beyond* the mind toward the light of awareness itself, "I" prior to any image. Eastern traditions focus on *the absence of desire*, since happiness is sought not in achieving particularly benign content to experience, but on stilling the quest for content altogether, allowing the happiness that is inherent in Consciousness to shine forth. This happiness makes itself felt precisely as movement and desire cease. These are broad brush strokes but they hold in general.

The sequence of practices I am about to describe begins with practices that make significant use of mind, and moves toward practices that make little use of mind. The sequence begins with simply finding the reins; thinking, yes, but in beneficial ways. This leads toward thoughts slowing and eventually stopping altogether, in silence and intimacy with the heart. The purification of content eventually gives way to purification of process.

Flash Quiz: Equations

Positive-thinking = (Western) Psychology = Fulfillment of Desire = Content = Astral Realms

No-thinking = (Eastern) Spirituality = Absence of Desire = Process = Causal Realms

The terms "astral" and "causal" realms will be explained in Chapter VII.

Technique

I will describe a number of different practices beginning with practices that use mind substantially, and move toward practices that use mind only minimally. This is a little like learning to play a musical instrument. In a sense, you need to learn to play and master the instrument of your mind. Many techniques are used in the process of learning an instrument. Different techniques are appropriate at different stages. You might begin with the repetitive practice of scales to develop manual dexterity, and to become familiar just with getting sound from the instrument. Later on, you might practice improvisation, allowing the spirit of the moment to spontaneously express itself, but this is only possible once mastery of the basics is acquired.

With mind, different techniques are also appropriate at different times. When the mind is racing and suffering is acute, it might be necessary to pull very hard on the reins to subdue the mind's racing. When the mind is quiet, less control and force is needed.

There will come a time when thoughts hardly arise from the mind. But it may be necessary first to pull hard on the reins until the agitation subsides and the danger passes. And, even as mastery is developed, states of mind will vary with the pressure life exerts, the challenges it presents, how hard your buttons are being pushed. In crisis, mind is more likely to panic and go awry. Mastery of mind is the ability to remain balanced no matter what life presents.

As a general rule, highly structured techniques are appropriate when the mind is racing. The mind needs a firm anchor to hold to when it is unstable. When the mind is quiet, little structure is needed.

Skiing, Again

I tried learning to ski late in life. The first skiing lessons I had were with a very skilled instructor. He gave concrete suggestions for controlling the skis, controlling speed, turning and stopping. I made good progress that first weekend and had fun navigating the beginner slopes.

A year later, I was assigned a different instructor. He was very Zen about the enterprise of skiing. He essentially said: Just flow with it, flow down the mountain, nothing could be easier. But I had no skills and if I flowed down the mountain, I would have flowed head first into a tree.

I am sure that what he said was correct, and would have been an excellent instruction if my skills were advanced to the point where flowing was the next stage in my development. But, at my beginning level, not only were those instructions unhelpful, they probably were dangerous.

Something similar applies to mastery of mind. The instructions that many great spiritual masters give is to do nothing, to stop doing. Effort suggests there is a distant goal to be obtained. But can peace be achieved through effort? Isn't peace precisely the absence of effort? And the goal is the here and now. How far away is that goal? No distance at all. No distance to cross. Any effort to gain what is already here only stirs the still waters.

Further, everyone is weary from effort and what we really need is rest, not more work, not something else to learn. Meditation practices are just more work. Absolutely true.

But what alternative is there when the mind is spinning crazily or when, like water torture, the mind drips and drips, thinks and thinks relentlessly? I believe it is useful to have practices that help to anchor the mind. When the mind is firmly anchored effort can be dropped, the very thing from which we need respite.

Floating Log

Each moment requires its own unique approach.
What worked yesterday is not appropriate today.
Like balancing on a floating log,
life requires continuous balancing,
in response to its changing movements,
spontaneous and intuitive responses,
and the gesture that was perfect to maintain balance a moment ago,
will only send you splashing into the stream if repeated.

Cognitive Psychology

The first practice of Positive-thinking we will explore is cognitive psychology. Cognitive psychology is a widely used psychological theory and technique that is used to alleviate depression, anxiety, and other painful emotions.

Cognitions are thoughts. In applying the principles of cognitive psychology, thoughts are examined for distortion or irrationality. For example, our friend, Jason, expressed the following thought, "Nothing is ever going to get any better."

Now, that thought is wildly irrational. *Nothing*, not one single thing, is *ever*, in infinite time, going to get *any*, not the slightest bit better? Pretty wild. In the language of cognitive psychology, the thought is irrational and includes many cognitive distortions that are well categorized by experts in the field.

The thought is obviously untrue. But if Jason buys into that story and makes it his reality, he will become despondent. His thought has a very bitter taste. Anyone taking seriously the thought - "Nothing is ever going to get any better" - must become hopeless.

Cognitive psychology provides techniques for adopting a more rational view. The more rational thought is already a form of Positive-thinking - a better thought. Jason must first recognize that his thoughts are irrational. He then has the opportunity to reevaluate. He might say, "Some things may get worse but some things must also get better, just by themselves. If I make a commitment to improve things, there is an even greater likelihood of success. And even if I do not succeed, is that the end of the world?" This is more rational, more in accordance with reality; a better thought with a better taste.

I will sometimes tell patients to listen not to the voice of doom and catastrophe but to the inner voice of compassion. Find a kinder voice within to counter the clamoring of fear. Try speaking with the kindness and tenderness you would use with your beloved child. Would you say to your child: "You fail at everything. You screw everything up. You are a total loser." And if you did say this to a child, what effect would these words have? Yet we speak to ourselves in this tone all the time; emotional violence, self inflicted.

Here is an exercise. If there were divine love, in your heart of hearts, what would you like to hear divine love say? How would the voice of love sound? Maybe something like:

Hello sweetheart,
How I do love you,
How precious you are, your smile and your humor.
I loved you before time as you know it began,
before the rocks formed and the wind blew over the face of the deep.
I rejoiced in you, for I know only to rejoice,
and joy is the song you too sing in your inmost heart.
Remember that song you once heard,
while your soul once swayed,
before you came to walk here amid the heather and the hedgerow?

Let your own heart sing for you need no other song.
Yours is the beauty for which the sun rises.
Yours is the beauty the stars attend.
Yours is the beauty for which winter compromises,
the fields wave,
the waves rush,
and the rushes bend.
Yours is the beauty the worlds have come to celebrate.

Find the voice of compassion and speak to yourself not with violence, but with love and tenderness.

Now, the very act of noticing and questioning thoughts, as cognitive psychology instructs, is the beginning of freedom. When you are hypnotized you take the hypnosis as real. You completely accept the hypnotic suggestion and so are completely under its spell. Once you look at a thought you are able to question its validity. You are outside the thought and spell.

Effectively you say, "Now wait a minute, hold on. Is that thought real? Is it true? Am I really a chicken? Do I really need her approval in order to be happy? Do I believe it? Do I want to believe it?" By questioning the suggestion, the hypnosis starts to wear off.

The importance here cannot be overemphasized. This insight, coming from the domain of Western psychology, begins the spiritual path. By not taking thoughts at face value, you separate yourself from mind. You are no longer embedded in mind. "You" are something other than mind. This process culminates in the ultimate spiritual question, "Who am I? Who is it that is aware of thoughts, or anything for that matter?" Not taking thoughts at face value is the first step in disentangling the Self from the appearances with which it has been identified.

If you can see it, you don't have to be it. Once you can look at a thought or belief, once you no longer simply accept the thought at face value, you have stepped outside the thought, you observe and so are no longer embedded in the thought, and don't have to buy into the story it implies.

Cognitive psychology, a dominant trend in Western psychology, would have you examine thoughts for rationality, correct the irrational elements, substitute a better, more rational and even more compassionate thought, and so change your mood. In this sense cognitive psychology applies the principles and is a first form of Positive-thinking.

Mandated Reporter

Diane tells me that she is demeaning and critical to herself in her thoughts. She frequently "beats herself up" in her thoughts, an often used phrase.

Diane, let me remind you that I am a mandated reporter. I will have to call Social Services and report you for abuse to your inner child! A report will be filed and your tender self will be removed to prevent further abuse from the inner bully. Or, if I call the police, you will be charged with assault with a dangerous weapon: your mind is the weapon, a power tool out of control.

Visualization—Guided Imagery—Hypnosis

Visualization involves an active mind that is consciously directed. You have hold of the reins and move thoughts in chosen, desirable ways. Your mind is exercised like an obedient, well trained horse, a horse that does not just run but goes where it is told. In the similar processes of visualization, guided imagery, and hypnosis, you tell yourself beautiful stories, or listen to the beautiful stories others tell, stories of heaven rather than hell.

The importance here also cannot be overemphasized. If I have a nightmare - say I am being chased by agents of evil who mean nothing but harm - I wake up with a start, my heart pounding. I was dreaming - pure imagination - but my body heard my mind and pumped adrenaline as if the dream were real.

So, if I can become genuinely frightened by imagining scary stories, I can bring about joy just as easily by consciously imagining stories of joy. If you can work yourself up, you can work yourself down.

Whenever I am miserable, I am probably telling myself miserable stories. To change from a mood of misery, simply remove the focus from misery to a focus on fulfillment. Imagine that your fondest wish, your deepest desires have come to pass. Imagine that you express your highest potential in the world. What would that look and feel like?

I suggest playing, "the imagine game." You may feel that life is cruel but, just for fun, imagine that life were kind. What would that look and feel like? You may be disappointed but, just for fun, imagine what success would look and feel like. The imagine game bypasses self-defeating tendencies to cling to disappointment and sorrow.

We now have two strategies in developing mastery of mind: defense and offense. Defense is the ability to resist or withdraw from Negative-thinking; good as far as it goes. Offense is the deliberate cultivation of positive images.

Attention is Miracle-Gro^{TM}, Innate Creativity. As with the light in the projector which spontaneously lends reality to any image placed before it, whatever you pour your attention on will grow as if by miracle. Stories of misery or stories of beauty: each will grow if attention is poured there.

We had a newly constructed front walkway and a newly carved patch of bare earth that needed planting. I chose plants for the new garden and encouraged them with liquid Miracle-Gro™. But the weeds in the soil were also fertilized. As the plants emerged, I had to be careful to pour fertilizer only on the desired plants, not to fertilize the weeds as well.

Whatever you give attention to will grow. Your mind is the garden. Be careful not to fertilize the weeds and grow a garden of negativity. The weeds will squeeze out the flowers. By giving attention to negative contemplations, you are actually choosing to pour the Miracle-Gro™ exclusively on the weeds. You will grow a garden of abundant weeds while the flowers wilt. Begin instead to cultivate the flowers, the thoughts of peace, beauty, and fulfillment and grow a beautiful mental garden.

The woman who was being hypnotized during childbirth was engaged in a process of guided imagery. She was being told a beautiful story - you are in a forest, the brook is babbling, you feel wonderfully peaceful. She so allowed herself to become immersed in the beautiful imagery that she became oblivious to pain.

There are many commercially available recordings of guided imagery or hypnosis. Often there is soothing music playing in the background. The music works like the induction in hypnosis, fostering a state of relaxation, so that the mind is receptive to the guided imagery.

I sometimes give patients the following visualization: Take some time, perhaps when you are in bed, relaxed, about to sleep. You are like a painter facing a blank canvas. Your life is the canvas. You can paint any picture or series of pictures. How do you want to picture your life? What would you want your life to look like? The canvas is blank, awaiting your creativity. Try to paint heaven on earth. What does heaven on earth look like for you?

This exercise is helpful to begin using mind as an ally. It helps to clarify the path someone might choose for herself, to discern the desired path to fulfillment. Imagining bounty also tends to create a mood of joy, for such is the taste of bounty.

One caveat. I am not suggesting that if I imagine myself as a rock star or President of the United States, that I will end up as a rock star or President of the United States. By imagining, I may feel the thrill (or terror!) of being on the big stage, but whether I end up on the big stage is more complicated than that. The hypnotized woman felt the peace of being in the forest while her thoughts were trained there. She may never actually go to a forest in her life experience.

As another example, there is a place on the Cape Cod National Seashore that is, to me, one of the most beautiful places on earth. I almost never see another soul there. The dunes are unspoiled, their contours carved by the wind, looking roughly as they may have when the Pilgrims first landed.

Rising above this landscape is just one lovely and tasteful house. How fortunate to own the house that presides over these solitary dunes and ocean!

I have at times imagined that I am lounging on the deck alongside the house which overlooks this exquisite landscape. I imagine the rush of the ocean and am lulled into a state of peace by the rhythmic crashing of the waves. The cries of gulls intermittently pierce the sky overhead, as do the roars of seals assembled by the hundreds on the sandbars. The sun in the cloudless sky bathes my body in warmth, while cooling breezes caress my skin and stir the seaside foliage.

I sink into relaxation imagining myself there. Mind is firmly in hand and serving the purposes of peace. Will I ever lie on the deck of that house? Probably not. Simply because I can imagine something does not mean it will materialize in my experience. Still, the image works to relax mind and body as I likely drift into sleep.

If I imagine a life of plenty, mind and body will be joyful. But who knows what plenty may actually come?

Conditions

I am not sure why things happen as they do. Why life turns out the way it does, why we face the situations and circumstances we face; that is a difficult question to answer. It can only be said that for something to happen, the entire universe must collaborate in its happening.

There are many New Age teachings that suggest that the images held within are simply out-pictured in your life. If you hold images of wealth, those images will materialize and wealth will appear. If you hold images of deprivation, those too will appear. It is as if life says, "Go create. Create whatever you wish, whatever you image. You are free to create according to your lights, for good or for ill."

This certainly is true to some extent. If I want to build a house, I must first imagine the house I would like to build, what size, what style, where I would like to locate this house and, if there is enough momentum, if the conditions are ripe, I may end up in the house of my imagining.

But the operative word is *may*. If I envision a mansion on fifty oceanfront acres in the Hamptons, I strongly suggest that house will not materialize. There are many recent teachings that suggest you can have and become *anything* that you envision.

These teachings potentially create the suffering they purport to relieve. I spoke to a patient who imagined winning American Idol - or a successful career in the music industry at least, a chart topping artist living the good life in LA. One imagined sailing the Mediterranean on her finely appointed yacht. Another was earning thousands of dollars a day trading the stock market, with the home and lifestyle to match. Unfortunately, these dreams did not materialize and hearts were broken when disappointment set in. The teachings suggest that the images of success must be held with conviction, so the disappointment was all the greater when the dreams were shattered.

I prefer the philosophy of conditions. This philosophy states what is perhaps obvious: something comes about when the conditions for its materialization are present. If the conditions are present for my sailing the Mediterranean on my sumptuous yacht, it will come about. But this most likely requires that I come from a wealthy family, have amazing talent in sports or the arts that brings enormous wealth, or that I create a web service that becomes a household name. Barring those circumstances, most likely I will never sail the Mediterranean in luxury. Not that it really matters.

New Age teachings will say I am being negative and this very negativity prevents my desire from materializing. Wrong. The desire will materialize only if the conditions are present for its materialization, and what does materialize does so because the conditions are ripe.

Now, the universe is infinite. I suppose it is possible, if I hold a desire deeply, that I may create the conditions for its fulfillment - but in some other maybe distant lifetime or parallel universe in a multiverse. If I desire nothing more than to sail the world with my yacht and crew, I may be born into wealth in some other life, century, or universe - if that is how things work - so that I can realize my desire.

My parents were Holocaust survivors. To say they endured the concentration camps because of negative thoughts is just rubbish. Rather, the conditions were present for those fates to be theirs. The conditions of their birth - that they were born Jewish, in a certain geographical location, in a certain historical era, with certain financial circumstances - innumerable influences brought those fates to fruition.

I can see how the experience of the Holocaust was essential in their life journeys. It is quite possible that the intelligence of the soul, for its own greater purposes, created the conditions for that fate. It is quite possible that we create our destinies more comprehensively than we now imagine. I just want to suggest that philosophies proposing that your thoughts simply materialize should be taken with a grain of salt; as much a setup for disappointment and suffering as for success.

If I have the means to build my house, it will be built. If I have the capacity to create the means, it will be built. If I simply imagine money materializing there must be some mechanism in place for that money to arrive. Yes, I receive checks in the mail when I send out insurance claims for services I provide in professional practice. I may receive checks for returns on investments I have put in place, if the investments are successful. Checks show up when there is a vehicle in place for the money to reach me, but the mechanism is not really all that magical.

Faith

The Boston Celtics have been beating the Orlando Magic in the 2010 basketball Eastern Conference Finals. It looks as if the Celtics will pull off another upset and defeat the Magic, as they did the Cleveland Cavaliers and league MVP LeBron James. I heard Dwight Howard, the center for the Magic, say that the Magic will still win because they have something the Celtics do not have: faith. Howard, a wonderful young man who does much public service, is a devout Christian.

But faith does not win basketball games; nor does faith affect outcomes in general. Outcomes are the result of the conditions in place. For most of the last century, Chicago was second in population only to New York, yet all the prayers from the vast Chicago population did not help the Cubs win the World Series once. Their teams simply were not good enough. What wins basketball games is the ability to put the ball in the cup. What creates outcomes are the conditions present for those outcomes to materialize. Whoever wins this series will do so because the conditions are ripe, the personnel in place to outplay the other team, faith or no faith.

Pie in the Sky

It is not uncommon to encounter self help teachings that promise unlimited abundance in every respect for all. I do not entirely disagree. Ramana Maharshi spoke of unalloyed happiness; still, he developed rheumatoid arthritis and died of cancer. The happiness of which he spoke was not affected by his cancer. He did not possess great riches or perfect health. In fact, he died with very few possessions, as did Gandhi. He spoke of the happiness of Self, an unalloyed happiness that is inherent in Consciousness, which persists in spite of adverse circumstances.

Suzuki Roshi, who contributed greatly toward establishing the practice of Zen in America, died of cancer. The ecstatic Indian saint, Ramakrishna, died of cancer but remained ecstatic. Many great saints, exemplars of spiritual realization, were not materially wealthy and became ill in ordinary ways. Great spiritual realization is apparently no guarantee that the body will not decay. The Buddha often pointed to old age, disease, and death as characteristic of earthly life. Still, Nirvana, the end of suffering, can be realized while on earth.

I wonder whether philosophies that promise unlimited potential in every respect for all set the stage for eventual disappointment. This is not to say that unalloyed happiness is not available, it simply comes from a different quarter.

Prayer

Let's take a different tack: prayer. Prayer is usually associated with religion but, understanding the mechanics of mind, prayer is actually a form of Positive-thinking. In prayer, the mind is elevated above mundane preoccupations in order to approach the divine. It is as if the mind changes clothing, removes its dungarees and dons linen, dresses in finery.

I learned prayer in childhood in a summer camp, where we would conform to the orthodox Jewish practice of praying three times each day. Each day, early in the morning, before the day was engaged, the camp would assemble in a simple wooden sanctuary where, in a mood both solemn and inspired, the Holy One would be addressed. Late in the afternoon, still dusty from baseball, we would remove ourselves from play to offer gratitude. At night, with the crickets singing, the moon and stars hovering, the day would end with the heart again rising to the Holy One.

I learned that prayer was to be undertaken with *kavanah*, concentration, intention. This was a prelude to the Buddhist meditations I would later learn. All meditation begins with concentration to stabilize mind and harness its power. Concentration is key: the determination to keep attention from simply flowing through the old, familiar, and unconscious channels.

The prayers I learned were all love songs to the divine that had been recited daily for hundreds and thousands of years. This was prayer not as ordinary discourse, not speaking to the divine as to a peer, but a confession of love, a loss of dignity in an intoxication of longing:

Beloved, for Thee anything;
my knees scrape the earth as I fall,
my face scrapes the earth as I bow,
allow me into your chamber,
my heart weeps,
keep me distant no longer.

The love songs of Tagore, the ecstasies of Ramakrishna, were heralded in my childhood by periods of Hebrew prayer interspersed with sport. I discovered the grace of athleticism in my body, and the grace of divine longing all at the same time.

O Holy One,
I have wandered for too long.
My throat is parched,
my eyes burn from the windblown sand.
Where in this endless desert is your tent,
where is there water to drink, fig trees,
and a place to lie down?

Be careful what you pray for. Apply the taste test; what is the taste of your prayer? Do you pray for the destruction of your enemies? This will only intensify hatred in your own psyche and further your own illness.

The same principles apply to prayer as to any other use of mind. Prayer is beneficial to the extent that light is applied to images of beauty. If I pray with desperation, I may magnify desperation. If I pray as a helpless supplicant, I may magnify helplessness.

I am not suggesting a theology where prayers are heard and are answered. I am not speaking of prayer as an attempt to affect outcomes. I do not know that prayer does affect outcomes, though the resonance of beautiful thoughts may indeed have subtle effects on the world. I am only concerned with the potential of prayer to beneficially affect the climate of the psyche of the one who prays; an elevation of mind toward the divine.

Saints

Sara is a devout Catholic. She has been terribly ill as a result of a brain tumor that required the removal of brain tissue. She hasn't been right since, understandably.

Sara has relied on her Catholic faith to help her endure the suffering of her damaged brain. She explained how her faith works. At times Sara will feel herself covered by, surrounded by Mother Mary's cloak, or resting on Jesus' wounded feet. She prays to the saints and feels the unique grace each saint represents.

Sara believes that Mother Mary is actually present in the room when called and, for all I know, that may be true. From my point of view, when Sara calls Mother Mary she brings Mary's image to mind, a magnificent image of love and healing. As long as this image is held with concentration, Sara attunes to the radiance of her contemplation. When she calls a particular saint to mind, she attunes to the resonance of that saint. She may feel the grace of aid with practical problems or the grace of commiseration, depending on which saint she calls. She attunes to the many shades of grace represented in the different saints. When Jesus is brought to mind, she feels God Himself in flesh uplift her spirit.

Loving Kindness Meditation–Rosary–Chanting

The practices described so far have all used the mind robustly to defuse negative thoughts and mood (defense), and then to actively reorient mind toward images of beauty (offense). The next series of practices retain the shift toward positive content, but they also work to restrain the activity of thought altogether. Restraining the busyness of mind is a process of anchoring, keeping attention anchored to a deliberately chosen focus. Using the term broadly, all the following practices are forms of *mantra*. A mantra is a specific thought or series of thoughts that are repeated inwardly; the mantra becomes the anchor to which attention is tethered. I will also use the term "mantra" at the end of this sequence to denote a single word or vibratory tone that serves to anchor attention. In the following sequence, robust or elaborate mantras will be considered first, with a gradual tapering toward simplicity.

While meditation generally falls in the category of No-thinking, there are forms of meditation that employ a shift similar to prayer. Buddhist loving-kindness meditation is one such practice. In loving-kindness meditation, a series of thoughts are repeated inwardly to the exclusion of other thoughts.

In meditation, one object, called the primary object, is chosen as a focus for attention. When attention wanders and the wandering is noticed, attention is returned to the primary object. Earlier we referred to meditation on breathing and we will again. In meditation on breathing the breath is the primary object. In loving kindness meditation, the primary object to which attention is anchored is not breath, but a series of thoughts. Typically the thoughts are something like: "May I be happy. May I be peaceful. May I be free from suffering. May all beings be happy. May all beings be peaceful. May all beings be free from suffering."

As these thoughts are repeated inwardly, feelings of kindness and a deep desire for the welfare of oneself and others - all humanity, all animals, all creatures, all beings in every realm - grows. The mind is absorbed in thoughts of love and kindness that are repeated, over and over, that serve as the anchor for attention, and other thoughts are refused. The heart opens profoundly. If "every thought you think, you do to yourself," you are now doing love to yourself, filling yourself with thoughts of love, kindness, compassion, and the taste of love is happiness.

In this practice, mind is still used but to one of its best possible effects. In cognitive psychology, visualization, and prayer, mind was used robustly but with increasing focus. There was generous thinking, but thinking was controlled and exercised as an ally, working for not against our purposes. Here the role of mind is even more limited.

A series of only a few thoughts are clung to. The brakes are applied to mind with greater force and its movement is slowed.

A similar practice is the practice of rosary or *japa* in the Indian tradition. Beads are used as a tactile aid to accompany the recitation of prayer-like sayings. The Our Father, Hail Mary, or other prayer or mantra may be recited. This is similar to loving kindness meditation in that a limited series of thoughts are contemplated to the exclusion of other thoughts. When the mind is wild, it may be helpful to use these practices that tie the wild mind on a short leash to a firm anchor.

Chanting is the repetition of narrowly scripted thoughts, sometimes with music. The chants are like lyrics in a song. The chant is repeated, over and over, and so gathers more and more power, like the power generated by musical theme and variation in a Bach fugue, or Stevie Wonder refrain. As the momentum of chanting builds, passion and ecstasy build as well. The force of attention is entirely gathered into the tonality of the chant.

Sunlight is hot but when concentrated through a lens can cause tinder to ignite. The dispersed, ambient heat is concentrated through the lens until a flame bursts forth. Dispersed attention, when similarly concentrated, turns the mundane life of distraction into a life of illumination. Concentration is key.

Affirmation

An affirmation is a single positive statement, the title of a very happy movie indeed. Contemplating an affirmation shines the light of awareness through a single joyous image. Like learning the lines of new script, the affirmation is repeated inwardly until the new script becomes familiar.

When an actor is given a script, she must get into character. She must study the script and her lines so as to more and more deeply understand and embody the new character. She must find the character within her own experience.

The affirmation is the new script. Working with affirmation requires learning the lines of the script and getting into character, finding the resonance of the affirmation in your own experience. To keep things simple the script is just one line long. Really, it is just the story title. This single image is simply doused with the Miracle–Gro™ of attention.

When I played tennis or softball, I would sometimes give myself instructions as I played, so as to improve an aspect of my game. I might tell myself, "Keep your eye on the ball." Or, "Hit the ball in the sweet spot." Affirmations are reminders to stay focused in a certain way, to keep your eye on the ball. The reminder focuses attention and keeps it from wandering.

But in life you are *always* at the plate. As long as you exist you're on, it's your turn, you are at the plate, at bat. Affirmations are reminders to stay oriented, in focus, to stay conscious, to keep your eye on the ball during the perpetual at bat of life.

Louise Hay is the master of the affirmation. Her popular book and video, "You Can Heal Your Life," include many wonderful affirmations. A woman interviewed in the video stated that she does "reps" with affirmations, just as she would do reps in the gym: 20 curls in the gym, 20 reps of an affirmation in her thoughts. She repeats the affirmation inwardly, mantra like, so that new neural pathways are carved in the brain, new channels for attention to flow through. Like practicing scales, the new thoughts become firmly established and easily accessible: the muscle memory of the mind.

The affirmation ties attention on a very short leash to a very firm anchor. The tendency of mind to drift into unconscious and dysfunctional patterns is restrained.

The following series of affirmations are from the chapter on "Success" in "You Can Heal Your Life:"

Divine Intelligence gives me all the ideas I can use.
Everything I touch is a success.
There is plenty for everyone including me.
There are plenty of customers for my services.
I establish a new awareness of success.
I move into the Winning Circle.
I am a magnet for Divine Prosperity.
I am blessed beyond my fondest dreams.
Riches of every sort are drawn to me.
Golden Opportunities are everywhere for me.

Alcoholics Anonymous similarly uses a number of slogans, tried and true anchors for the mind that can be used like affirmations, reminders to keep your eye on the ball:

One day at a time.
Keep it simple.
Live and let live.
Let go and let God.

Mantra

The bridge between Positive-thinking and No-thinking is mantra. A mantra, in the way I am using the term here, is a word or very short phrase that is repeated inwardly. When the mind wanders into other thoughts and the wandering is noticed, the thoughts are refused and attention is brought back to the mantra.

There is a tuning fork on a table in my office. In the days before electronic tuners, I used the tuning fork to tune my guitars. I would strike the tuning fork causing it to vibrate, the vibration would hum to an "A," and the "A" string on the guitar would be tuned to that tone. Anything the tuning fork touches - the table, a chair - will amplify the tone by vibrating in sympathetic vibration to the tuning fork.

In a sense, you are always striking some tone in mind which creates the mood of experience. The tone might be "life sucks," or "beauty is everywhere." The mantra is a tone that is deliberately struck in mind; mind is as if tuned to the tone of the mantra. As the tone becomes familiar, as new neural pathways are carved in the brain, it becomes easier to access the tone and mood of the mantra. The default tone and mood of mind is reoriented. During the course of life, if the mind starts galloping, the galloping can be restrained by remembering and holding to the mantra. With practice, like a cultivated plant, the mantra becomes well established in the mental landscape.

A good mantra to begin with is the word "peace." Depending on preference other words - health, wealth, love, God, grace, truth, joy, purity, compassion, kindness, success, benevolence, plenitude, generosity - can work equally well. Say the word inwardly as if throwing a pebble into a pond. Let the resonance of the word - "peace" - ripple within. Attune to, hold to the feeling of "peace," get into character, and keep thoughts from wandering elsewhere. When the ripples subside, again say the word, throw another pebble into the pond, and again let the ripples spread.

The practice of mantra has been used for millennia in the East, and has gained popularity recently in Western traditions as well. For example, some schools of Trappist monks practice "Centering Prayer." In this tradition, the mantra is called the "sacred word." (Keating, Thomas. Open Mind, Open Heart).

The mantra can be coordinated with breathing meditation by saying the mantra inwardly on the outbreath. This practice has been called the Relaxation Response by the cardiologist and mind-body researcher, Herbert Benson. Benson coined the phrase the "Relaxation Response" to contrast with the "Fight or Flight" response. "Fight or Flight" occurs when, in response to threat or danger, adrenaline is pumped into the organism to prepare for battle.

We saw in visualization that the body and mood respond to the thoughts held in mind. Relaxation can be induced by focusing on images of the forest or ocean. If thoughts of danger are held in mind the organism will ramp up unnecessarily. This is the basis for anxiety: a self-induced and unnecessary feeling of danger. Like an engine that idles too fast, the organism will wear itself out by remaining in this heightened state. Holding the thought "peace" in mind is a reminder to relax and to keep other thoughts at bay.

If you can work yourself up, you can work yourself down. If you can create anxiety by harboring thoughts of catastrophe, you can create relaxation by striking a tone of peace instead.

Mantra is perhaps the best use of mind: mind pointing directly to the heart. Mind points out the quality of heart - "peace" - to which you would like to attune. The mind serves up the reminder - like striking the tuning fork - and that quality vibrates inwardly between repetitions of the mantra.

"Heart" can be used as a mantra. When I use this thought, it reminds me to orient toward the heart, to locate the center of my Being, the point of balance, and to settle into the inherent bliss that radiates from the heart.

You might try the word, "perfection." By viewing life through a lens of "perfection," you may see this moment as perfect. The universe is an expression of unfathomable intelligence. By viewing life through a lens of "perfection" you may release any demands on this moment, as well as the assumption that perfection is not present because the universe has not fulfilled all your desires and expectations. You release craving and dilemma and surrender to the beauty that this moment does express.

I like the word "wealth" as a mantra, a focus on plenty rather than lack. Unhappiness is usually an attunement to lack of some kind. Wealth is the opposite, a focus on presence rather than absence. "Wealth" involves seeing the glass as full rather than empty, acknowledging the abundance that *is* present in the moment, rather than focusing on what this moment seems to lack.

Jean Klein, a master teacher, talks about the mind state of "welcoming." By using the word "welcome" as a mantra, you might remind yourself to have a welcoming attitude toward life, to embrace, to be open, inviting, to allow all things, to be uncontracted rather than contracted, tight, clenched, or demanding in your relation to life.

Thirty or so years ago, a friend told me that, when he took LSD, everyone appeared to him as a god or a goddess. He would perceive at the level of archetypes. I have, when speaking with patients, used the word "archetype" as a lens to focus my attention, and so see each person sitting before me as a divine manifestation, a Hero or Heroine, a unique expression of divine beauty engaged in an epic encounter with life.

If love is happiness, a very simple mantra, especially for parents, is to repeat your child's name inwardly and, as you do so, feel the powerful, unconditional love that you feel for your child. You can similarly say the name of a spouse, parent, friend, or acquaintance as a form of loving kindness meditation. By recalling those that you love, by using their names mantra-like, it is easy to refocus attention and generate feelings of love and well-being.

I have imagined that I was in the company of the "master." Ramana has said that the guru is the one you trust, the one for whom the heart opens without qualification. For me, this is either Ramana or the Buddha, but it could equally be Jesus, Mary, St. Francis, Amma, Yogananda, or Ramakrishna; whoever it is you trust, whoever is the face of the divine. I repeated "master" inwardly and imagined myself actually in the presence of the Buddha. Is there anything happier than to be in the presence of perfect love and wisdom?

I have practiced elaborate mantras in Sanskrit or Hebrew. These mantras ask more of the mind and may be useful when a complicated task is needed to provide a firmer anchor for racing thoughts.

In practicing mantra the mind is slowed almost to a halt. Just one tone is struck in mind with each recitation of the mantra, and fullness of heart resonates in the aftermath of the striking.

Kindness

She had one child, Jane, before they married. He adopted Jane when they married, then they had two more children together. He and Jane never got along, there was never the bond he felt with his biological children. Just before I saw them for their initial session of marital counseling, there had been a big blowout and his wife was fed up.

He and Jane barely spoke, other than to acknowledge each other with little more than a grunt. If he thought of Jane, he immediately associated her with frustration.

As we spoke about the situation, his life as a whole and their crumbling marriage, he cried and softened from the mood of the blowout with which they had entered. He was receptive.

In the course of the day, I suggested, I want you to think "kindness" to yourself. Your mantra now, know it or not, is "frustration." You are pouring your attention on "frustration," growing a garden of frustration, you walk around fuming, and no one wants to be around you, an angry, sulking presence. I want you to close the door on frustration, to not entertain thoughts and feelings of frustration and, instead, say the word "kindness" to yourself in the course of the day. Every now and then, return to the contemplation of "kindness."

I also want you, in the course of the day, to think of Jane and to wish her a successful and prosperous life. Wish her well in your thoughts. When you see her, try thinking the thought "kindness," which will become an increasingly familiar thought and feeling. When you see Jane, stay focused by telling yourself "kindness," as you would tell yourself to keep your eye on the ball. Relate to Jane through a lens of kindness and see how the relationship is transformed.

Acknowledge Divinity

I was meditating and the mantra that came to mind, the keep-your-eye-on-the-ball thought, a good one, was Acknowledge Divinity. With that mantra, I was directing myself to acknowledge the imminence of divinity, to keep attention focused on the imminent divinity that might go overlooked in the preoccupations of mind. The effect of the Acknowledge Divinity mantra was to open deeply, inwardly to fall off a cliff and into a vortex, drawn down and drowned in an endless sea of spirit.

You want directions to Boston? Here they are: Acknowledge Divinity. The moment you do so, you're in love, you're in Boston.

To Acknowledge Divinity is to surrender to the presence of the divine in this very moment. You *are* the presence of the divine.

You *are* the presence of the divine. Where you are, the divine is. You are the Light of Being. Where you are, God is.

To Acknowledge Divinity is to say Yes to this moment, whatever may be on your experiential plate. Say Yes and the search is over. Say No and suffer.

To say No is to resist. To say No is to say divinity is not now present. In saying No, the heart closes and the inevitable Yes is postponed.

The fish is in the ocean and searching for the ocean. To say Yes is to acknowledge: Yes, this is the divine ocean. I am in the ocean. Not only am I in the ocean, I am ocean. There is only ocean, only divinity, only joy, only God. Melt into Truth. Even pain, when it too is acknowledged as divinity expressing itself, without any resistance, does not interfere with joy.

The taste of truth is joy. Acknowledge Divinity in this very moment, as your own Light, say an unqualified Yes, and the truth is found and its taste is bliss.

The Combination is Found

The combination is found,
the tumblers click into place,
the lock releases,
the door to the heart swings open.

Rescue Remedy

If you are feeling badly, know it or not, you are probably thinking badly. It is helpful to have some anchoring contemplations in reserve to turn to in a heartbeat when necessary. Just remind yourself to change the channel, and turn to the positive rather than the negative channel.

The rescue remedy for the mind is some affirmation or mantra that resonates within and strikes a chord of beauty. Construct a statement that represents well-being, or use affirmations from other books or these:

I am blessed by God.
I am an expression of divine perfection.
I am safe in a loving universe.

If you are feeling badly you have taken your eye off the ball. Use an anchoring thought to regain conscious control, rather than allow the mind to gallop unconsciously. *Choose* your thoughts rather than allow unconsciousness to choose them for you.

Choose an anchoring thought and *hold* to it. Stay with the thought; *do not allow the mind to wander.* It will wander into unconsciousness, the well worn, already carved pathways. This requires intent, determination, concentration to keep attention on task, to stay awake rather than falling back into the unconscious sleep. All meditation begins with concentration, which really is an issue of how intent you are to wake up and find your way out of suffering.

Thoughts that taste of joy are in accordance with truth. Say the thought inwardly as if throwing a pebble into a pond, and allow the impact of the thought to ripple within. Like striking a tuning fork, strike the tone in mind and, as if tuning yourself to the tone of the thought, resonate in sympathetic vibration.

Let's start with the first affirmation above: *I am blessed by God* (or *I am blessed by the universe,* if you prefer).

Say the thought inwardly as a way of grabbing the reins and getting the galloping of mind under control. Hold to the thought. Do not allow the mind to wander back into unconsciousness. The thought serves as the primary meditative focus.

Get into character. Feel the feeling of being blessed by the universe. Imagine that the blessings of the universe rain down upon you. You are loved. Your deepest longings are fulfilled in the blessing, your deepest desires come to pass. Your heart fills with joy and gratitude.

As contemplation progresses the mind quiets down. When this happens, the work that the mind does in reciting the affirmation may seem cumbersome. The mind wants peace and rest. So the affirmation "I am blessed by the universe," may resolve into its essence, "Blessed."

At this stage, the mind has quieted to the point that it does not want activity, and a simpler task is required to keep focus. The affirmation resolves into a mantra: "Blessed."

The warmth and fullness of blessing is present in the silence between recitations of the mantra. The heart is present in the silence. Bask in the glow of blessings, the glow of your own heart. The fullness of silence radiates now in the foreground, the mind having receded to the background.

You see, Positive-thinking solves the problem of negative *content* but not of *process.* While Positive-thinking changes the content to thoughts of beauty, the problem of process remains. The mind is still somewhat busy. As long as the mind is busy, tugging on the reins by holding to positive thoughts, work is still going on. The mind wants peace, to be free of work. The mind, the ego, wants to be submerged in the heart.

So there is still "work" to do. The mind must subside having settled into the heart. Then the problems both of negative content and process will be solved. For this we must consider No-thinking.

The Taste of Truth is Joy

If you can work yourself up, you can work yourself down. If you can generate panic by imagining catastrophe, you can generate bliss by imagining heaven.

If the mind is to be used, use mind in the best possible way. Cultivate a verbal or visual thought that has the taste of joy. I may imagine that I am lying at my favorite spot on Cape Cod by the ocean. I have all the time in the world and nothing to do but relax. I hold to this image. Once I relax sufficiently, the life current which had been constricted in a knotted up mind and body has space to circulate. Once the life current flows, like ice floes melting in warm currents, the knots dissolve and the body is bathed in a biological bliss.

Here is another image that may help. My wife brought two kittens home from the animal rescue. One of the kittens, Charlie, was very skittish at first. We believe he was mistreated as he did not trust people. We meant him nothing but love and kindness but his own defensiveness kept the kindness at arm's length.

We have all received blows from life's cruel hand and are all on guard and defensive. But for the purposes of contemplation imagine that, like the kitten in the loving home, life intends you nothing but love. You have only to open and trust to allow that love in. Relax your guard; it is no longer necessary. Imagine that you are safe in a loving universe, as Charlie is perfectly safe in a loving home. Imagine benevolence; nothing to fear. Imagine a universe of grace. This will tune the mind to a contemplation of love and safety, the body will relax and the armor will dissolve.

Since love is happiness, another way to generate happiness is to contemplate love. Using the mind as an ally, think of someone you dearly love and hold the image of this person in mind. As soon as love is located you will feel happiness. Hold to the image and let the feeling of love grow. Then think of someone else you love or have loved. Think of the many people you have loved in your life. Extend this feeling of love beyond your closest friends to the kid that sat next to you in first grade, your third grade teacher, the cab driver in the city, the woman at checkout in the supermarket. Extend the feeling of love to all.

In doing so the mind is being used purposefully. It is not allowed to run dysfunctionally but is harnessed to good end. Concentration comes into play, the ability to keep mind on an intended course. There may be visualization as you imagine those that you love, but a focused visualization as attention is held to love alone. Like mastering an instrument, mind is played masterfully to create the desired effect.

Contemplating love is sure to generate happiness. Love is joy. By contemplating love and generating joy, the chiropractics are lining themselves up correctly. You come into harmony with the nature of things, with truth, as the taste of truth is joy. When joy flows you are on the track of truth. Follow that track as far as it goes.

CHAPTER IV

INTERLUDE – STORIES

D*ear reader: We are pausing our tour here to browse in the shop of stories.   A bag lunch has been prepared.   Please exit the bus single file and collect your lunch as you exit.   You may browse the shop at your leisure, selecting any story you like for your personal collection.   When you are done browsing, please board the bus and take your seat.   Our tour will resume in the next chapter.*

A. Clinical Vignettes

What follows are impressionistic vignettes I wrote following sessions with patients, as time allowed.   In almost every case, the patient embodies some form of Negative-thinking - and consequent suffering - that must be restructured, and the vignette suggests a possible restructuring.   Often the negative lens on the world is a result of early conditioning.

If you have blue sunglasses on, everything looks blue.   If the *cognitive* lens through which you view the world is blue, negative, then the world looks blue, but only because that is how the world is being filtered.   I try to perform soul-chiropractics in each case by suggesting cognitive adjustments, crunching the cognition, so as to bring the patient's world view into better alignment. I may suggest a rosier, more harmonious lens through which to view life, and with that adjustment suffering should abate. These are forms of Positive-thinking. No-thinking awaits.

Self Denial

As a child he was abandoned first by his father through death,
then by his mother through alcoholism.
Desperately alone, a child bereft in an imposing world,
he peopled his loneliness with voices from within,
and took solace in the church and the promise of salvation.

As an adult he longed to be a religious,
a solitary monk,
to leave altogether the imposing world he never quite mastered,
never quite belonged to.
In order to make himself worthy of this vocation,
he felt the need to perfect humility, self-effacement, self-denial.

This is anorexic thinking.
The one already thin and hungry thinks himself not thin enough,
thinks himself opulent, in fact,
and deprives himself even unto death,
a pure distortion of perception.
The one already denied all the nurturance a soul needs,
thinks himself imperfect in the way of denial.

Rather, be gentle.
Love yourself in every way,
serve yourself in every way,
find comfort where you can.
You may find joy more congenial,
than a bed of nails and a beaten breast.

Boundaries

As a child she picked blueberries in the woods behind the house. There was a rock that seemed immense, but which may have been immense only to a child's eyes. (I remember a rock like that from childhood, a rock in New York City; how big could it have been)? She knew not to go beyond that rock and into the woods. She feared going beyond the boundary and being lost. She remained within the cocoon of safety bounded by the rock.

At one time, as an adult, she felt safe only within the cocoon of her bed. The world beyond the bed seemed frightening and unsafe. Eventually she made it out of that bed and allowed the cocoon to expand into a circumscribed world, a small town. But there was always a boundary, even if indistinct, beyond which a threatening world loomed.

Allow the cocoon to expand to encompass the universe. Let the boundary of your Being expand limitlessly. Let there be no beyond. The world beyond the rock, the world beyond the bed, the world beyond the town, it is, all of it, You.

Mirrors

She could barely walk in the door and see her husband without anger bubbling up. The anger was always there, raw and close to the surface, a hair trigger that took only the slightest provocation to discharge.

Thank your husband, I said. He is your teacher, showing you where you have buttons that are not yet dismantled, where the capacity for ignorance and suffering remain. You walk in the door and the anger is instantly there, stimulus and response. You see him only through the lens of your conditioning, the lens of memory and the past, never afresh.

Life constantly holds up a mirror so that you can see yourself in each situation. Each moment and every situation discloses to you the status of your evolution.

Resentment

In couples counseling, the counselor may try to get the combatants to look past their negativity, to remember the purity of love that was present at the outset, when love was seen in the other's eyes, and could only lead to eternal vows.

For the individual sometimes the same change must be effected, so that love is seen when looking outward toward life, the same love felt when the soul, like the marriage, was innocent and the world was new, before disappointment set in and life, like a faithless spouse, was resented.

Thawing

Throughout his life people had treated him cruelly. In childhood he was the target of bullies who beat him for entertainment. His own parents undermined his confidence; at night, from his bed, he could hear their derision. Like someone in shock, like someone freezing, when blood abandons the extremities and collects around the heart and vital organs, preserving life at the expense of the more expendable, his energy had collected in the interior of his soul, preserving what integrity remained after the physical and emotional assaults.

The year my youngest child was born, I did not have the time even to try to rake the leaves off the lawn before the snow fell. When the snow melted, the grass was all but dead beneath the blanket of soaking leaves. But I was told, "The seeds of life survive below. Water, fertilize, trust; it will revive."

His spirit, like the bed of grass, was all but smothered beneath a blanket of abuse. But within, huddled around the warm bloodstream, the essential spirit of life survived, needing only a thaw, enough nurturance, reassurance, encouragement, love, to dare to sprout again innocent into the sun.

Reprieve

Though life may have been disappointing, and one's fondest dreams have proven hopeless, as insubstantial as the morning mist and as likely to come to fruition, there is nevertheless within oneself a sacred flame that has been neither touched nor extinguished by life's rejections. There is a flame that *cannot* be extinguished, and in that flame is a happiness without form, without condition, it is the perpetual happiness of Being; look there and not simply to the promises of fortune.

Maya

Francesca is involved in a relationship that began like fireworks; their first date never ended or, rather, it ended with his moving in. They have been together almost continuously since. But the inevitable complexities of life are damping the flames, and there are few dazzling trails left marking the sky. He is embroiled in a custody battle from a previous marriage, the kids are in his charge for the summer, he left Francesca suddenly to be with the children, and has barely communicated since. The fantasy, the stroke of amazing luck, has given way to abandonment.

The situation brought to mind the last chapter of Hermann Hesse's masterpiece, The Glass Bead Game. In that chapter, "The Indian Life," Hesse describes the twists and turns in the life of the protagonist, Dasa, his journey from the sensuous intoxication of the marital bed to hatred, disgust, and murderous rage, as fortune smiles favorably, before fortune disappoints and betrays.

I dreamt that night that I climbed to the summit of a mountain ridge and, in the distance, where the mountains yielded to the plains, opalescent on the horizon, lay the City of the Orient, shrouded in a dusky fog that played on her minarets and spires like eyes revealed, then drawn back into secrecy. Music broke over pointed scales and wafted into the night, like perfume rising from a woman's throat. And as I looked out on this vision I was lost and knew I had next to meet this lover, hopelessly entranced and yet apprehensive of the knife I sensed hidden in the veil.

Dasa discovers the variability of life, the seductive illusion of Maya, as destiny takes him from the riches and privileges of royalty to the bitterness of war, capture, and the death of his son. All this rise and fall is Maya. Francesca, too, has been subject to Maya's fickle duality; a dream come true, eaten unknowingly from within, crumbled.

Relying on anything in the realm of change is dicey. Fortune rises and falls, for such is the nature of duality. That being the case, like a boat on stormy seas, one's anchor needs to be set into the deep, moored all the way down to the ocean floor so, while the boat on the surface may rock, the anchor remains firmly planted and the boat can drift only so far. One's anchor needs to moored in the eternal, the unchanging. When that is the case, though the storm and seas may rage, the rocking of change can have only so much impact. Absent this, the boat is at the mercy of the storm, and will drift and crash with the whims of the wind. One's anchor must be planted in the eternal for happiness to be firm; then let change do what it will.

Landscapes

Her mood had changed. She had been an actor and dancer and knew herself as passionate, expressive, with feelings close to the surface, even raw. But now she noticed she had become detached, with no investment in outcomes, with no strong feelings, whatever came about was cool.

Have you ever driven across the continent? There are definite regions - coast, desert, mountains, plains. There is transition as one landscape changes into the next. She had experienced a landscape of passion, a landscape with great peaks and valleys like mountains, but as she kept moving that landscape changed into something less turbulent, something more level like the plains. There was something benign in the level terrain, and something left to be desired.

As life moves this level landscape of detachment too will change; the flatness will eventually yield to terrain altogether different, yet to be discovered.

Mania

She had a manic episode or so the criteria call it. I think she had a glimpse of reality. She walked up to the people whom she would meet in the course of her daily life and thanked them for the gifts they had given her, with their smiles, with their very presence. For the first time, she entered the house of the woman next door and they talked. She gave money to people on the street and said, "This is not my money, it is God's money." Yet this action - giving money away - is seen as by far the most irrational behavior, the surest sign that she is mad.

She is called manic and I suppose she is, but perhaps she also has broken the bounds of convention, the handcuffs of social norms, and is free in some way that is to be envied, studied, appreciated, questioned, learned from, not simply condescended to and suppressed under a blanket of tranquilizers, until the conventional perspective is reestablished, and any ecstasy broken.

Questioning

He too was diagnosed bipolar.
He found himself weeping at work for no reason.
He left work and began to question - everything.
The marriage he was in for so many years,
to a wonderful woman, a wonderful friend,
but something had long ago left the relationship,

and he questioned whether to stay married.
He questioned his career in business;
was the work still meaningful,
or would he rather be in human service?
He questioned his world view,
moved tentatively toward the conclusion,
that the world really was religious in nature.
He questioned his own judgment and capacity for normalcy.
Online he met someone from the West Coast,
with whom, uncannily, he shared almost everything.
He decided to visit her, questioning his capacity for decision making,
was this a true decision or was he simply being manic?
His parents pointed fingers,
to reinforce the fear they had always taught,
but he questioned their teachings.
He made the decision to visit his new friend in California,
and had one of the most meaningful episodes in his life,
perhaps the first time beyond the wall of fear he had lived behind.
His life had come to that pitch,
where everything was open for question,
no situation or value to be retained on inertia alone.
He stood at the threshold of a new and frightening world,
a world of great promise and great terror.
He faced a great moment of truth;
a great opportunity to remake himself under the star of authenticity;
was it that or was he simply being manic?

Paranoid

She is paranoid, afraid of the world, so chronically abused that she considers all people abusive, out only for themselves, and by this assumption undermines what help people of good faith may choose to give her. Her own view precludes the love she seeks; then she blames the world for its failure to love.

Oriented

She worried that if she did not worry, who would? If she relaxed her guard, if she did not stay constantly vigilant, would things fall apart? Wasn't it necessary to worry to keep disaster at bay? Isn't it necessary to think to stay on top things? How can one function without constant thought and worry?

You are oriented in space, are you not? You do not need to tell yourself over and over: I am in Central Massachusetts, Boston is east, New Hampshire is north, California is west. No, you are innately oriented within space and time. You know where the grocery is, where the airport is, and what steps are necessary to get there.

You know where you live. You know how to start your car. You know where the keys are. Do you need to worry about finding your way home? Do you have to remind yourself how to eat a banana, or how to open a door?

You are globally oriented. You do not need to remind yourself about the situations you face, your relationships and their status, who is in your family, when to pay the bills and how much they might be, what needs to be done with this or that situation. It is all already known in your being oriented.

Allow yourself to be present, don't obsess, and respond to situations as they present themselves. Life will take its course. By being present you will respond to situations fully, appropriately, and not simply react from conditioning. You are deeply oriented within life. You know your way around. Trust your innate intelligence to respond to situations without forethought or obsession. And in being present there is the opportunity to taste the sweetness that life may hold.

Oedipus

Allen's parents always fought and eventually divorced. His mother could not help but share with Allen, as a confidante, the extent of her contempt for his father. Through sympathy with his mother, Allen came to agree that men are fools, to be denigrated. As we speak I try to help, but Allen is quick to contradict and denigrate whatever I may say. What I say is faulty; and here is a better way to look at the problem.

Remember, Allen, that you are creating the climate of your psyche; in this case, denigration and contempt. You are free to continue in this vein but your thoughts have a bitter taste, and this lens on men will defeat not your Oedipal adversary, but yourself.

Buried Treasure

Clay came into the office severely depressed. He cannot tolerate work any longer. Like a boxer being pummeled in a fight, the ref needs to step in and the fight stopped before it brings Clay to his knees. Certainly, let's fill out the paperwork for a leave of absence.

I often quote the Serenity Prayer:

God grant me the serenity to accept the things I cannot change,
The courage to change the things I can,
And the wisdom to know the difference.

It takes wisdom to discern when a situation needs to be changed outwardly or inwardly. If wisdom suggests that an outer change be made, by all means make that change. If no outer change is possible, then an inner change, a deepening of acceptance and serenity is in order.

I know Clay well and know that he has negative programming going back to childhood. The work situation, his boss in particular, triggers that programming. If there were no programming, no button to be pushed, the situation would not be as dire.

So take some time, Clay, heal, and we'll revisit things in a while. The bus is barreling down the pike; let's get out of the road. I know that Clay wants to travel, to see Europe, India, wants a companion; may all those blessings come to pass.

But here is a suggestion for Clay and in general. Consider that happiness does not come about from acquisition. Happiness is not to be sought in the future by gaining something that you do not now have.

When I look at my own life, in my twenties, I wanted to travel to Asia to live as a Buddhist monk and meditate. I did that. Then I wanted to attend graduate school at Harvard. I did that. Then I wanted to marry, buy a house, and have kids. I did that. I have a great wife, a great house, and great kids. Has any of it fundamentally solved my problem? Has the pursuit and fulfillment of desire through the better part of a lifetime fundamentally solved my problem? No. Nothing acquired ever solved my problem.

Many people want relationships, join online dating services to meet someone, and often they do. They are now in relationships. Is their problem fundamentally solved?

So here is an experiment. Consider that happiness is not found by pursuing desire. It is not found in the future when circumstances change for the better. It is not in the new relationship, the new job, or the new house. Lots of people have relationships, jobs, houses and their problem is not fundamentally solved. They are still searching.

Consider that happiness is a buried treasure that is available in this very moment of existence. As you read these words, you are in possession of happiness but it is buried in the quiet beneath the mind.

This moment is the place to look to find the lost keys, not the attempt to acquire something you do not now have. Look to this moment, eternally to this moment. Where to look? Your heart. You *are* the buried treasure. Happiness is buried at the heart of Being.

Change

She said: I feel nothing. I care about nothing. Even though I have been trying for six months no change has occurred.

Six months ago it was winter. The trees were bare, the ground was frozen and covered with snow. Now it is spring, almost summer, the leaves miraculously are filling in the trees, it is warm and pleasant outside. I can turn my face upwards and feel the welcome warmth of the sun.

If you step into your backyard and look at a leaf today, and look at the same leaf tomorrow, you will say that there has been no change, that no movement has taken place. But clearly there is movement. The difference between the outdoors today and the outdoors six months ago is extraordinary, an entirely different landscape. From today until tomorrow, however, on that one leaf, no change seems to take place. Change is subtle and seemingly imperceptible. But as your observation becomes keener, you will notice what is now imperceptible, what now passes below the threshold of your observation, only because your observation is not sufficiently keen.

Become like the student botanist who measures with great interest the size of the leaf each day. Each day, on her graph, she records the slight differences in the leaf, and the graph displays enormous change over six months. You too are in movement. Only pay more careful attention, look with more care, and you will feel what you do in fact now feel, and how you are in fact now moving.

Don't Hang Out With Doubt

Tom is a talented young filmmaker, just graduating from college. He has already produced public service announcements that have aired on TV. But the process and prospects of "making it" seem daunting. He needs to secure an internship, there will be lots of competition, the competitors may have better skills, it can seem overwhelming. Tom, I said, don't hang out with doubt.

"Don't hang out with doubt." I like that, Tom said. It sounds like your parents telling you not to hang out with a negative influence, like the kid with firecrackers and Swiss Army knives.

Tom also worries about the relationship he has been in for two years, how that will weather the transition from college.

Wasn't it Freud who said that the major components of life are Love and Work. As you graduate college, Tom, and embark upon your adult life, you are worried about both components, Love and Work, your relationship and your career.

I have always added another component to that formula: Self. Life is Love, Work, and Self: your relationship with yourself, how healthy you are, how consonant in your Being, how comfortable in your own skin.

Love and Work are the contents of life. Self is the context. If your relationship with your Self is whole, if you are consonant within your Being, you can make your way with wisdom through the contents of life: Love, Work and whatever else life may hold.

Conditioning

Heidi posed an interesting question. Her adopted son, now a teenager, struggles with serious mental illness. It is hard to imagine that he will ever be free of his mental illness. Heidi herself suffers from depression. She reflected on their respective states of mind and began to wonder if she too could ever be free of her depression. Just as her son will always be subject to his mental illness, would the same be true for her?

At one time Heidi made her living grooming and training dogs and knows animals well. Speaking in those terms I said: Heidi, some dogs are compliant and easily trained. Other dogs, by breed and temperament, are much more difficult to train. But some training is possible in either case. Training, however far it may go, will only help matters. The mind is similar. Your son may be capable of only so much progress; your mind has fewer biological limitations. Like someone recovering from a stroke; clearly the brain has been wounded. How much functioning can be recovered, where the biological boundary is - as with other biological diagnoses like ADHD or OCD - is difficult to know. It is difficult to say what gains can be made, but gains are possible in all cases. Training the mind can only benefit and we will see how far it can go.

Hitchhiking

The job he worked at for the last several years became unbearable. The job seemed like a good idea at first, good retirement and benefits, but the day to day work was numbing. Now middle aged, he would look for some other opportunity. There was a possibility at the ski lodge; or he knew someone who owned a company and might have something available. He could study design in school and open his own business, or could finish his degree and become a teacher.

I used to hitchhike and have crossed Europe and the Western U.S. by thumb. When I had time to travel, I realized there were two ways I could approach hitchhiking. I could choose a destination and only take rides that brought me closer to my destination. Or, if an interesting person or set of circumstances presented itself, I could go wherever the ride led.

He approached life taking whatever ride came his way. The effect was not to get anywhere in particular. Each situation lasted as long as it lasted; then he had to start anew. There are many ways to go about life and that is certainly one option. Just be aware, if there is some specific goal, some value, desire, or aspiration in mind, most likely it will never be attained.

I Don't Care

Andy has been using drugs consistently since he was eighteen. Lately his drug of choice has been Oxycontin; it's feels cleaner than heroin. He does not use every day and hasn't used in a couple of days. He is psychologically, not biologically addicted. When asked if he wants to help himself his answer is: I don't care.

Andy, the "I don't care" thought keeps you in a fog. As long as you take "I don't care" seriously it is acceptable to withdraw from life and self destruct. "I don't care" must be rejected whenever it arises, the voice of the devil.

As long as you believe the "I don't care" thought it is acceptable to abuse narcotics, to avoid work and social interaction. Once you reject that thought, refusing it whenever it arises, you will experience an enormous depth of caring, the very caring you had to defend against by going into the fog. Your feelings will thaw and you will return to life.

Substance abusers love the high, the relief from suffering that drugs and alcohol bring. But the objective in life is purity in mind and body; the ultimate high. Substances appear to provide relief but only create deeper impurity and so more ground to cover, more obfuscation to be cleared before the heart can be revealed.

No Escape

It is well known and often stated in the treatment of substance abuse that you cannot escape from problems through alcohol or drugs. Problems need to be dealt with. Substances provide a temporary escape but, in the long run, the problems remain with the additional problem of addiction to be resolved.

It is also true that you can't escape from your mind. You are stuck with yourself. You are never exempt; there is no way away. And just as there is no escape from problems through substances, there is no escape from yourself. The only solution is to authentically deal with mind by making it a congenial environment in which to live, by resolving mind into quietude.

Shifting

She asked: Why can I not seem to get beyond this? Why do I still suffer?

We look outside the window. It is a cloudy day. There is a thick layer of high clouds and the sun is completely obscured. If we did not know better, we would not know there was a sun at all.

You are like a plane that is flying *within* that cloud layer. You continue to fly horizontally, the way you have always done, and are surrounded on all sides by clouds and obscurity. You are not making the vertical shift, taking the altogether new direction that will bring you above the clouds into clear and beaming sky, where the sun is radiantly apparent. You insist on continuing in the familiar way, in spite of the fact that the known way is also known to be unsatisfactory.

Wise Response

Robin had a difficult childhood which left her fragile, though she has been able to manage through life. However, during the last three winters she needed to take leaves of disability as her depression mounted in the darkest days of the year. And her divorce put in her in a position where she is entirely responsible for her financial needs.

This year, Robin is not recovering well from her winter leave of absence partly because she has many additional stressors. Now divorced, she can no longer afford her mortgage and has put her house up for sale in a down market. She is filing for bankruptcy. She was instructed by her psychiatrist to attempt a return to work - an ambitious plan, I thought - and today sat in the parking lot at her place of employment for her proposed return, unable to bring herself to enter the front door. Later, she came to my office.

Robin is in a panic and the panic is disabling. During the winter sabbatical, she essentially hid in her rural home, in denial of the crisis about to crash down upon her. Eventually the situation descended, her house went into foreclosure; there was no more denying that the wolf was at the door.

She does not understand how it is possible to acknowledge loom-
ing disaster without panic. She is judgmental, feels like she has failed,
but the fear and failure just disable her more completely.

Robin, I said, I am not a fan of denial. Pretending something
does not exist when it does is not the path. Pretending there is no bus
speeding toward you will lead to disaster. No, a bus is fast approaching and we need to respond. But to panic as the bus approaches and
to blame yourself for being in the road only disables your ability to
respond. Those reactions are at the heart of the disability.

The question is: how is it possible to acknowledge that there is a
situation needing wise response, how to acknowledge the crisis without going into panic and blame? Can you respond to the crisis with
compassion and kindness for yourself, and for all you have undergone?
Then you will deal with the situation from a climate of compassion,
kindness, and forgiveness toward yourself. You must hold the reins of
mind tightly, keeping it on the course of kindness, so as to use this
situation for learning and the benefit of the soul.

Religion

Charles and I have been discussing spiritual ideas for quite some time.
Only recently did he inform me that his religion deems all these ideas
mystical, mysticism is heresy, and must be avoided.

Religion paradoxically, tragically, may make it absolutely certain
you will go in the wrong direction. By following its dictates you may
be sure to get nowhere near the divine.

Charles, let's go Testament. One of the commandments in the Bible is, "Thou shalt have no other gods before me." This means that your primary consideration should be of God. When your thoughts go elsewhere, when other considerations arise, return to the remembrance of God.

However the practice is framed, the primary mechanism of practice is remembrance, the act of waking up. The simplest meditation instruction is: focus attention on breathing and when your mind wanders, bring attention back to breathing. This requires withdrawing from thought and coming back to the primary object, the breathing. This mechanism is at play in virtually every self help and spiritual practice: withdrawing from unconscious preoccupations.

The primary object may vary. The focus may be an affirmation, a mantra, the breath, the body, but in each case withdraw from thought and remember the task at hand, however the task is framed.

Cult

Her father was a monster and the child literally feared for her life. She learned from this monster that she had no worth, and that life was a frightening place, always ready to punish. She learned not to express herself for to do so was to risk humiliation.

You know members of cults - the Moonies, Hare Krishnas, and others? They are all programmed with distorted information that they believe is true. They live their life assuming a falsehood is real. When they are separated from the cult, they must go through a process of deprogramming, where their distorted beliefs are exposed and they assume beliefs more in line with reality.

Your family is like a cult that you are born into. In the cult of family, you may have learnt all kinds of distortions. Now that you are separated from your family, your beliefs need to be adjusted, brought more into alignment with reality. The world need not be punishing; it may fulfill your dreams. And your worth, well, that is beyond measure. Any real father would remind his child repeatedly of that truth.

Parenting

Attention, he ordered his daughter. In the Marines for twenty years, his work was to transition young men into manhood and he would do the same with this teenager. There were rules and penalties for breaking the rules. She started throwing up. You are ordered not to throw up! She threw up more frequently.

A child is a flower with which you are entrusted. The flower will bloom in its own time, in its own way. There need be no fear that the flower will not bloom, for such is its nature. The parents' job is only to tend, to water, to aerate, to nurture the blooming along, and to stand amazed when the flower buds and blossoms into its innate beauty.

Purity

Ever since Catherine had her baby her OCD has been out of control. She washes her hands more than fifty times each day, and she hovers near the baby to make sure that no one else's germs can get close.

But Catherine, I said, while your hands might be very pure, your mind is not pure at all. Unlike your hands, your mind is deeply soiled, stained with fear. And it is this impurity of mind - fear run rampant - that is behind your compulsion for purity elsewhere. You are trying to assuage the mind's fear by washing your hands. But no amount of washing is sufficient because fear, the source of the problem, is not addressed. No amount of antibacterial soap will wash your mind clean.

Forget purity of hands. Undertake purity of mind. Try to discover a mind - not a hand - that is pristine.

Catherine leans forward on the sofa as we speak to make no contact with the seatback where others have sat. Her mantra whether she knows it or not is: "Contamination lurks everywhere." That is her ever present contemplation and its taste is anxiety.

But Catherine spent her life in theater and dance, so I give her the lines of a new script and ask her to practice these lines and get into character. The lines that the character in this new role speaks: "I am safe in a loving universe." Catherine, please practice these new lines, not by rote but get into character, feel the mood of the one who says: "I am safe in a loving universe." She admits she gets a good feeling when she repeats these lines inwardly.

God's Will

George witnessed an industrial accident. It was a normal day at work, nothing out of the ordinary, George was on the machine beside a friend and, just like that, the friend's clothing caught, he was pulled into the machine and was instantly crushed. George looked up and there was his friend, bound with metal strapping, spinning on the rod like any other piece of cardboard.

Despite every effort and treatment modality, George cannot shake the anxiety. He knows that, at any moment, something can go horribly wrong, if not for him then for his family or someone he loves. He lives in fear of the next catastrophe.

George's terrible contemplation is, "Disaster is about to strike." He is a practicing Catholic so I suggested that he use the mantra, "I accept God's will unconditionally." Inwardly say: "I accept God's will unconditionally." Life is uncertain and things can be upended in a flash. Death will come in its time, perhaps suddenly and unexpectedly. But if acceptance of God's will - the universal will - is deep, one can live in peace despite uncertainty. One can look out to the world and see nothing but God's will being done, not just in catastrophe, which is rare, but more commonly in the bird's song, the leaf's flutter, the rain's patter. To surrender unconditionally, to lay down all resistance to God's will is to live in peace.

The Evolutionary Imperative

Dave is a smart and talented guy. As a kid out of high school, he was admitted to Penn in the Ivy League. But his family was never supportive and, here again, withheld the support that would allow him to attend college. He managed on his own to train in architecture and built a business that brought in six figures. Then his young wife died. Since then, years now, he has mostly been lying on the couch, drinking. His attitude is basically, "Who cares, why bother?" This attitude, taken to its logical conclusion, is suicide: Why bother living at all?

Dave, life is structured with a built-in Evolutionary Imperative. Evolution is moving like a stream toward the ocean. The individual and collective are moving inexorably toward Higher Consciousness; call it Enlightenment, or God. That is the inherent movement of life, a movement that cannot be defeated. You are immersed in the stream. You can hang onto a branch and resist the movement forward. But, eventually, the pain of hanging onto the branch, resisting the flow, will force you to release your grip and you will surrender to the stream. The flow toward the infinite ocean is the Evolutionary Imperative; built into the structure of life. It can be resisted - painfully - but can never be defeated. Surrender and the pain of resistance will be transformed into the joy of fulfilling your potential, and your destiny.

Stories

There are stories told in books, theater or film that, however well told, are nevertheless stories without consequence, stories without reach beyond the momentary entertainment. When the story ends there is no residue, nothing left over, no pondering or change of heart, no need for reflection or discussion, no moral lesson. With the story's end, so ends the story's significance.

Greater stories, on the other hand, have import, meaning, one leaves the story illuminated, edified, wiser in some way. Friends or scholars may gather for hours or centuries to discuss the story and its implications. One's ponders the layers of meaning.

Life is itself an ongoing story. We are all protagonists in the stories of our lives. And the nature of life is that the story we live has complete import, perfect significance. The story of the life we live is utterly saturated with meaning, for the story is the vehicle of personal transformation and enlightenment.

B. Journal

The next two sections are like journal entries, reflections; I am my own patient here.

The Greatest Pleasure

While cross country skiing in the White Mountains of New Hampshire, I stopped on a remote trail to look out at the woods and reflect. I was alone, and the pine forest was dusted with new snow.

My father-in-law used to say that vacations were designed to exercise lots of mortal sins: gluttony, lust, and sloth among them. We had done our part to sin well on this annual winter getaway: delicious dining in town, and relaxation in our secluded, third-floor room back at the inn.

So among these pleasures, and the pleasure of vigorous exercise in an unspoiled wilderness, stopped on the trail I asked myself: where is the greatest happiness to be found? There is happiness in superb food, in rest and intimacy, in physical health and vibrancy, certainly. But the greatest happiness and what is most satisfying, I realized, is a quiet mind, a mind free from its grappling with life, a mind at peace.

Papaji, a disciple of Ramana, used to say: I need you to quiet your mind for a period of time equal to a finger snap. Why did he ask so little? Because that finger snap requires, for one moment, that the entire movement of time and mind, the entire immersion in story and becoming be relinquished, and that the imminence of the moment, of stillness, of Being be tasted.

Stop for one moment trying to get somewhere, step outside the time-bound story, and taste this moment. This is perhaps the greatest intimacy - with one's own Being - and the greatest pleasure.

Touching

Spirituality is about intimacy. It is about touching. Touching this moment. Touching one's Being; touching the Being of another. Touching, with awareness, one's body. Touching the pain and the knots inside one's body and, by touching, allowing those knots to dissolve. Touching fear for, in touching, there is an overcoming of fear; fear is avoidance, the unwillingness to touch. What one seeks ultimately is an end to the feeling of disconnection, one has scarcely recognized from what. Spirituality is all about coming into contact: with oneself, with this moment, with others, with life, entering into communion, becoming intimate, touching.

Training

I have been running lately, getting back into shape now that spring and the warm weather have returned. We live in hilly country. There are formidable hills around every corner. At first, the hills were overwhelming and, halfway up, I would bend at the waist, panting and struggling. Then, as some strength was developed, I began to attack the hills with a sense of confidence and challenge, watching my tendency to bend at the waist, and would return upright when I noticed my vigilance and discipline relaxing.

In life too the terrain is varied. There are flat, easy stretches and then formidable hills. The hills may seem overwhelming, like periods of great adversity that force one to bend at the waist, to pant and struggle. But seeing the hills as opportunities to build strength changes attitude, until the hills are appreciated as tests to gauge, as mirrors in which to view capacity, to see where immature tendencies are retained and reactivity, non-strength remains.

My Mother's Dying

First day of spring,
and what a winter it has been.
It has been the winter of my mother's life.
The leaves have fallen off her frame,
her frame is bare and broken from the weight of snow.
I have thought, while watching this process of decay,
even if there were a God,
well, prayer is certainly worthless.
Why is it the Western world makes such a big deal of prayer,
and researchers try to find correlations between prayer and healing?

Were there not many prayers prayed during the Holocaust?
Were there not many prayers prayed,
during every atrocity human beings have undergone?
Were there not many prayers prayed,
by every person gone bankrupt in one way or another?
Yet the Western world elevates prayer,
imparts it with great value.
I think instead of the Indian sage who said,
"Whatever is destined not to happen will not happen,
try how hard you may;
whatever is destined to happen will happen,
do what you may to stop it.
This is certain.
The best course therefore is for one to be silent."

There it is.
What will happen will happen,
in spite of all the prayers prayed to prevent it from happening.
Children of devastated parents will die,
economic recession will descend, as it does now,
the cycles of victory and defeat will persist.

First day of spring.
Victory is on the ascent.
My child saw the first leaves of the first crocus this morning.
The snows of winter are melting under the gathering sun;
no prayer for winter can possibly prevail.
The winter of my mother's life approaches,
she shivers under the gathering cold.
First day of spring for the earth,
the snows of winter deepen within her ailing body.
Say what you will,
no prayer can prevent either.

And if no prayer can affect outcome,
it is fitting only to retreat into silence,
into the heart before any hope is hoped for,

prior to the entire turning of the world,
with its seasons of hope and despair.

He said yesterday that life is pain.
You are a Buddhist, I told him.
This life may be painful in the season of pain,
but the world of seasons is just one occurrence,
in a much greater context.

That is the essence of religion, is it not?
The essence of religion is the belief that,
in spite of appearances,
in spite of painful death and having to watch painful death,
(I think it might be easier to bear than to watch,
those one loves bear painful death),
in spite of the appearance of meaninglessness,
there is meaning;
in spite of the appearance of lovelessness,
there is love;
in spite of the appearance of indifference,
there is care;
in spite of the appearance of being adrift,
there is guidance.
The essence of religiosity, of faith,
is the intuition that behind it all,
there is *something* rather than nothing.
And all religions give this something a different name -
God, Nirvana, Self -
but all basically say the same:
behind the appearance of suffering there is beauty.

First day of spring.
The birds are making their seasonal appearance.
Is it hope that I hear in their calls or am I projecting?
Do I actually hear in their calls the voice of that *something*,
that abides beyond the veil of appearance, or am I projecting?
Do I hear in their calls the voice of the object-of-faith,

the voice of the beyond,
and see the shape of the beyond in the trees and sky,
and feel the touch of the beyond in the wind on my cheek,
or am I projecting?

I hear the voice;
I see the shape;
I feel the touch.
The warmth melts the snow with which my heart has been encrusted,
watching winter overtake my loved one,
but these messengers of spring remind me,
that behind the appearance of death there is everlasting life.
Suffering may have its place;
it, like all earthly life, is a moment that will pass,
and pain remembered is no pain at all.
The pain will pass, spring will return,
but this will be a spring everlasting,
a spring without end,
a spring without season,
a spring that grows ever beyond itself.

Behind the appearance of temporality,
there is the eternal.
Behind the appearance of limitation,
there is the unlimited.
Behind the appearance of pain,
there is freedom.
Be still; it will all be revealed,
when the season of turning passes.

Eulogy

Sitting by your side,
witnessing the early stages of your dying, Mother,
I feel death is more a process of saying thank you,
than it is a process of saying good bye.
Because there is no good bye, I believe.

I believe in the eternity of life and love,
and know I will feel your presence whenever I call.
So rather than interpret death as loss,
I would rather celebrate a great soul and a great love,
the great gift of our relationship,
the unfathomable bond between two beings.
Death, then, is thank you as much as good bye,
an opportunity to celebrate love as much as to grieve its loss.

Thank you, Mother.
How can I thank you for the purest love I have been given?
For life has often been unkind,
and I have felt to life an afterthought, incidental,
of no great merit or importance.
In the midst of this indifferent life,
a life that I could take or leave,
as easily as life could take or leave me,
in one place I always mattered,
and that place was You,
and its face was Yours.

I think back upon my life,
a life you always helped along,
and remember my childhood, adolescence, and maturing as a man.
I see the patterns of success and failure, optimism and defeat.
I see the overview, two acts of the completed play.
I see the thrust of my life forward,
its aspirations and pursuit of dreams.
Mostly those dreams were rewarded,
but sometimes dreams were battered down.
I think of a toddler learning to walk,
standing excitedly, taking some wobbly steps,
before crashing butt down, cushioned by a diaper,
pausing just one moment to absorb this unexpected turn of events,
before leaping forward once again.

That is life, isn't it?
We are toddlers until death, aspiring, falling, aspiring.
You sit hunched in your geriatric chair,
your fractured bones too painful to lie on,
sedated with morphine.
You were on your way to Florida for the winter, leaping forward,
had already sent your bags along.
One wrong movement,
and the weakened edifice of your body crashed.
But, like the toddler's crash, this too is temporary.
At the very least, with death, you will rise again,
into a new and freer life, enthusiasm restored, horizons open.

Even now you give a gift,
it seems your blessings never cease.
Your death awakens me to my love.
Never have I cried so deeply and completely.
The snow has been falling abundant and often this winter.
With each snowfall the earth is made new, pristine,
the landscape is a sea of white.
With each fresh falling of tears my soul is made new, washed clean,
purified, innocent as snow.
I think you bear your pain as one last gift, O Mother,
and thank you, thank you, and bless you on your journey.

Pat's Dying

We went to visit Pat today. She has been given a life expectancy of
up to three months as her body fills with cancer. There are tumors
on her brain and liver. She was groggy from the narcotics and not in
control of her faculties. I was familiar with the discussion of pain killing drugs, for my mother has been taking the same drugs and is also

losing her faculties. At first, I could not tolerate sitting alongside yet another hospital bed, and found myself inwardly moving to silence, so that the painful scene would be outside the purview of judgment.

When I was a Buddhist monk in Sri Lanka, undergoing the stages of suffering that arise classically in the course of Buddhist meditation, I realized the only way out of the perspective of suffering was to make no judgment.

I wrote:

"If God is that which is utterly worthy of praise and thanksgiving,
then it is also true that He is utterly worthy of contempt.
For as much as we may derive joy from the unbidden miracle of life,
equally may we be horrified at pervasive and innocent suffering.
And all suffering is essentially innocent,
for man cannot considered responsible for his ignorance."

But not to rail for those dying on the Calcutta streets, not to rail, but to sink into a place of non-judgment, of absolute internal stillness, that sees and accepts life as it is. I was reminded of that insight sitting there with Pat.

I have been playing music lately and find my fingers moving beyond the known, beyond the familiar scales with their familiar emotional intonations, into a music that is evocative though I do not understand why. The music is beyond my understanding, beyond what I have known music to be, and I have to relinquish the known to play and allow the beauty of this music. With the smell of death in the bedroom, or reflecting on collective death, I must leave the familiar and settle into an unknowing, a non-understanding that allows life to be what it is, without consciously understanding and without judgment.

When we left Pat to sleep her husband, Barrie, said, "We bounce along in the material world undisturbed until something like this happens, and then have no choice but to flow with a deeper current."

An Open Field

The long weekend skiing in the Green Mountains of Vermont had ended, and I drove on ahead of the family. When I arrived back in town, I went first to retrieve our Golden Retriever, Max, from the kennel where he had been imprisoned for four days. First things first, Max and I drove straight to the conservation land where I released him. He bounded with such incredible glee at having finally been set free. He ran and romped and rolled on his back in the snow, lapped water at the edges of the ice, where the pond was melting in the January thaw. I have never seen any creature so exuberant, so celebratory. Okay the walk is over, Max, back in the car, back to the house, where the message machine disclosed that, over the weekend, our friend Pat had succumbed to cancer.

I only hope the joy that Max displayed, released from a cage in a stuffy kennel, to a beckoning, wide open field, quilted with snow, with room to roam and roll and play, is the same joy the soul feels when it is finally released from the physical.

C. The Buddha

Darwin and the Buddha

He believed in the scientific method, in Darwin, and the absence of meaning. Evolution moved of its own. But he also believed the Buddha and had great faith in the possibility of salvation from suffering.

What are the implications for a world so constructed that Nirvana is within the human capacity, is in fact the essential human nature? Does it not say something that human evolution culminates in happiness? If the world were as the existentialists have described, and there were no inherent nature, no inherent bliss, truly an argument could be made for meaninglessness. But a world destined for happiness; what does that imply for benevolence in the greater scheme?

The Four Noble Truths

Physics is an attempt to discern the ways that the physical world works, how the forces of nature hang together to yield the familiar world we inhabit.

The language that expresses the relationships among the forces that physics studies is symbolic, mathematical. A simple formula or equation may actually be a statement of thundering insight into the elegant orchestration of energy that is the universe. The physicist is like a mind reader; the equation is the idea read from the mind of God. The physicist's quest is to read deeply into the cosmic mind, to enter the inner sanctum, thereby to be made privy to mystery.

But while an understanding of the physical world is important - for pure knowledge and its implications, philosophic and practical - it seems even more important, if such exist, to understand the laws and principles that govern human existence. It is one thing to see into the workings of matter; it is quite another to see the meaning, reason, and redemption of human existence.

Two thousand five hundred years ago, Siddhartha Gautama, a young prince from Nepal, sat to look within his own Consciousness for the meaning of human existence. He vowed not to move from where he sat until he attained the perfect illumination he had determined eons before to attain. The evil one, Mara, feeling threatened by the steadfast prince, fearing the diminishment of his own dominion attacked, hoping to deter Siddhartha from his resolve. Mara exercised all his power for desire and fear, trying first to seduce then to discourage the prince, but Siddhartha could not be moved. In response, Siddhartha pointed to the earth, witness to the sacrifice he had undergone in preparation for his destiny, this moment. Mara was defeated. Then, unimpeded, penetrating all obstruction, Siddhartha turned his eye more profoundly inward and looked into the heart of the universe.

In the first watch of the night, Siddhartha saw his thousands of prior lives come and gone. I was called this and died thusly, he recalled. He understood that other beings too are caught in endless cycles of becoming, never resting, never still, never sated. The wheel of birth and death, though insubstantial, turns mercilessly, he thought, shot through with suffering.

In the second watch of the night, he understood that deeds have consequences rewarded in kind. Noble deeds yield happiness, evil deeds unhappiness. Seeing humanity founder, seared in the fires of passion, his compassion grew even greater, for there was no security to be found anywhere in the illusory world of Samsara.

In the third watch of the night, he saw the causal sequence which perpetuates the process of birth and death. Ignorance has consequences: Consciousness incarnates in a body which is possessed of sensation; sensation leads to desire; desire leads to attachment; attachment to renewed existence. But with the cessation of ignorance the chain could be broken. There was freedom to be won with wisdom.

In the fourth watch of the night, Siddhartha ascended to the pinnacle of illumination, attaining perfect realization, becoming a Buddha, an enlightened one. It is said the denizens in all the heavens rejoiced; joy spread through every realm. Everywhere the momentum of virtue strengthened; everywhere the event reverberated.

After remaining seated in bliss for seven days, Gautama Buddha, out of compassion, rose to teach. He encountered the ascetics with whom he had earlier practiced. The ascetics regarded Siddhartha with suspicion, for he had taken food and so had abandoned the asceticism they cherished. Why did this one, who catered to his body, approach?

But the Buddha's radiance was undeniable, hypnotic. The ascetics recognized the light of freedom in his eyes and listened.

The Buddha spoke and so set the wheel of truth in motion in the world. He spoke the essence of his enlightenment, the Four Noble Truths. Herein is the formula of thundering insight, springing from the heart of life, the supernal vision, the sublime.

The California Marriott

We flew to Southern California for a magnificent wedding,
the reception held in a resort high on cliffs overlooking the Pacific,
as the sun and moon set over the blue ocean.
The plane flew over the red desert,
over the Grand Canyon and Rockies where,
above tree line, crevices were filled with snow.
As we flew over desert, canyon, and mountains,
a B movie and reruns of the Brady Bunch,
played on video monitors in the aircraft cabin.
Most everyone stared at the monitors,
while the crowning glory of the continent passed below.
The last time I flew it was night and the aurora borealis,
the northern lights filled the sky,
but the mostly business travelers did not look up from their work,
so mundane I suppose was the event compared to their briefcases.

In California we stayed at the Marriott.
My daughter wanted bananas for breakfast.
I bought bananas at the coffee kiosk each day.
I noticed each day that the bananas were perfect,
served only on the day of perfect banana ripeness,
yellow but firm, unspotted, unblemished,
cut perfectly from the bunch,
with perfect stem and perfect curve.

I remembered this tale.
The astrologers told the king,
father of the infant prince who would become the Buddha,
that his baby would be either a great king or a great religious figure;
it was not yet clear.
The king wanted an heir,
and so did everything to keep the boy,
blind to the travails of the world,
that might awaken his religious calling.
The prince was kept in a palace where everything was perfect;
no wilted flower, no withered maiden,
only the young and ripe, the beautiful and strong.
That story no longer seems mythical for now,
perfect flowers, perfect fruit, perfect meals, perfect pools,
an altogether perfect world,
is available not just to a prince in an ancient fable,
but to anyone staying at the California Marriott.

The Transcendental

Legend has it, the astrologers suggested two possible destinies for the child, Gautama: either he was to be a great king or a Buddha, an emperor either of the world or of the otherworldly. And, in fact, these same two alternatives present themselves, archetypally, to all who feel the inner urging of perfection, to all who long for the mystery of Being to yield up her secrets, and strive to bring out of the inchoate, the sublime.

But the question becomes: does one recognize the superficiality inherent in phenomenal experience, however profound, however abstract the experience; does one see that the attainments of genius are not waters enough to give drink to the fill of the soul and so, tenderly but with resolve, as one would leave a lover behind, turn from the worldly and toward the transcendental?

CHAPTER V

NO-THINKING

Q: Are good thoughts helpful for Realization? Are they not... a lower rung of the ladder to Realization?

A: Yes, this way. They keep off bad thoughts. They must themselves disappear before the state of Realization.

Q: But are not creative thoughts an aspect of Realization and therefore helpful?

A: Helpful only in the way as stated before. They must all disappear in the Self. Thoughts, good or bad, take you farther and not nearer, because the Self is more intimate than thoughts. You are the Self, whereas the thoughts are alien to the Self... Are you not distinct from thoughts? Do you not exist without them? But can the thoughts exist without you? (Talks with Ramana Maharshi. P. 256).

This quote from Ramana Maharshi points to the threshold between the psychological and the spiritual realms. Positive-thinking is a series of practices within the psychological realm, where mind acts favorably upon itself, turning from an enemy into an ally. But the spiritual realm goes beyond mind to the simplicity of Being. Thoughts, good or bad, extend from You, from the Self, so the Self is more intimate than its thought productions. The spiritual realm is about settling into the heart prior to mind. This is not about changing the content of mind from negative to positive, which is a good first step, but about subduing the process of mind altogether. When there is no process or activity of mind, there are neither negative nor positive thoughts. Only Being remains, the context within which thought and everything else arises.

Review

As we transition into No-thinking, let's review the ground we have covered so far and glimpse the ground ahead.

We started the journey with unconscious negative thinking: bad thinking on automatic pilot, a recipe for personal and collective suffering.

Thinking can be negative either in process or content. Negative thinking in process is a mind that runs, a mind that is always busy. I will look carefully at some patients in therapy sessions and notice in their eyes, if there is even a momentary pause, that mind wanders immediately. It may be to something innocuous - what groceries need to be bought just after the session - but the busyness never rests. It is almost impossible for the untrained mind to stay still for a moment without preoccupation.

Negative thinking in content, however, is a mind that dwells on matters inherently painful, like fear of the future or failure recalled from the past. These thought-behaviors tend to create anxiety and depression.

We began to apply conscious control, to harness the mind, so that mind cooperates with rather than undermines our purposes. We did this first by redirecting thoughts in cognitive psychology. We decided not to take thoughts at face value, to question the validity of irrational thoughts, and to substitute a more rational and compassionate perspective. In doing so, we started the process of creating order out of disorder.

Withdrawing from negative thoughts is defense. Next, we began to play offense, to purposely cultivate positive thoughts. When mind is to be used, let us use it well. If attention is Miracle–Gro™, we decided to pour attention on and so to fertilize the flowers and not the weeds. Mind was active in visualization and guided imagery, where elaborate scenarios of beauty were imagined.

In prayer, mind was similarly active but its contents were elevated. Prayer is mind directed by heart.

Then we pressed harder on the brakes. In loving kindness meditation, rosary, and chanting, a limited series of thoughts or prayers were contemplated repeatedly. In affirmation, a single sentence, and in mantra a single word or idea were contemplated. As mind slowed, its process restrained and content consciously chosen, the light of awareness shone unmediated in the presence between thoughts; the sun peeking through the clouds.

Now we will subdue the mind more significantly in the practices of No-thinking. We begin to prefer the silence from which the thought emerges to the thought itself.

No-thinking can be broken down into dualistic and non-dualistic phases. Dualism involves a subject contemplating an object, and is "dualistic" because of the inherent "two-ness," the subject and object. Non-dualism is the last and highest stage we will consider.

In continuing to move from chaos to order, we will first consider duality and then non-duality, the state of the greatest order, balance, and sanity.

Jackhammers

She thinks obsessively and has always considered herself a worrier. "I can understand Positive-thinking," she said, "but have no clue what No-thinking might be."

Imagine that you live next to a construction site and jackhammers pound away all day. You are so accustomed to the noise that you almost don't notice; you take for granted shouting across the living room to be heard above the din. Then dusk descends, or the project is completed, and the jackhammers cease. The noise stops and it is quiet. That is what No-thinking is like. You are so accustomed to the inner noise it almost seems like the natural state, like someone who assumes jackhammers are a way of life. But obsessing is not natural, that is why it is painful. Quiet is the natural state and a welcome relief when it arrives.

Talking or Listening

Thinking is *talking* - talking to yourself - talking "in your head." Thinking is actually talking inwardly; no one else hears the conversation but it is a conversation - a state of talking - nevertheless.

There is a saying: Prayer is when you talk and God listens. Meditation is when God talks and you listen.

You can either be talking or listening. You cannot do both at the same time, though attention can move rapidly from one to the other. If you are talking - to yourself, thinking - you are not listening. In order to listen, talking needs to stop. This is meditation, becoming inwardly still, entering the state of listening.

So there are two modes, the talking mode and the listening mode. The talking mode is the state of thinking, talking to yourself inwardly. The listening mode is meditation, or what has been called *mindfulness*, which means being present, being aware, paying attention, listening to the life before you. Jean Klein has called this the state of *welcoming,* where you are open and allowing of whatever life presents.

The entire discussion of Positive-thinking involved variations on the talking mode. As we move into No-thinking, however, we leave the domain of talking and enter the domain of listening.

The following was mentioned earlier but bears repeating. A thought arises. If you do not think the thought along, if you do not enter the conversation, if you do not enter the talking mode, thinking does not proceed. The initial thought bubble bursts and that's that. Thinking proceeds only with participation, only if you enter into and further the conversation by leaving listening and entering talking. And thinking occurs only when there is inter- est in the conversation. Once interest is withdrawn, the story and conversation end.

One difficulty with listening is that we enjoy our dramas. We find them engaging, even compelling. We like to think because we enjoy our story lines. There is something delicious about it all. We especially love being right, as opposed to the other idiots who are just so wrong. We love the inner conversations where we tell the others how it really is, and we emerge victorious. There is something delicious in all our fantasies or we would not continue to fantasize. There is even something compelling about fear, loneliness, and depression, so much so that it is difficult to stop those painful thought processes. It is all so very delicious.

There are two difficulties in withdrawing from the inner talking. It is delicious - we enjoy our fantasies - and it is habit. Like water flowing through the ancient riverbed, mental energy flows through its well worn pathways of thought. It therefore requires keen awareness to keep the familiar habits of mind from simply reasserting themselves. This keen awareness is the state of listening. If you are listening, talking does not proceed because mental energy is diverted from those pathways. Your stance shifts. Your center of gravity is as the listener, the observer of thinking - and all else - rather than as the one embedded in thinking.

Everyone is aware of the need for exercise to keep the body strong. But the mind also needs strengthening. Meditation is like taking the mind to the gym. A strong mind is a stable mind, a quiet mind, its buttons - its reactivity - dismantled, a mind disaffected of the habit to think and react, and so not tossed about on the waves of life. And the primary exercise for the mind is to be aware, to listen, to abandon the talking mode and remain in listening.

Mindfulness

Mindfulness is equivalent to the listening mode. Being mindful means being present, noticing what is taking place, being here and now. What prevents being here and now? What prevents mindfulness? Only the reassertion of the talking mode - thinking - which takes attention away from the here and now and toward the elsewhere. So if you are trying to be mindful, simply remain as listening; notice (listen to) what is present. The present may happen to include the arising of thought, that is, the arising of the ego as the thinker. But if you are attentive, thought cannot persist once it arises; thought persists only with participation. By withdrawing from participation in the talking mode and remaining as listening, you are practicing mindfulness.

Yoga

I have taken a number of yoga classes, the first when I was a young man. Even with a youthful body, I found the postures difficult. The teacher would say, "Bend down, keep your knees straight, touch your toes. Now place your palms on the floor." That was the beginning; it got worse. At the end of that first class I approached the teacher and said, "I can't do these exercises. I'm not cut out for yoga. I'm just not flexible enough." She answered, "That's exactly why you need to take yoga. The exercises are designed to help you develop the flexibility that you lack."

I am often told with regard to meditation, "I can't meditate. I'm not cut out for it. My mind is too restless and unruly. My mind just races while I sit. I can't concentrate. I want to get up and do something." My answer is the same: "Meditation is an exercise in getting your mind under control. The fact that your mind is unruly is precisely why you need to practice. If you were perfectly at peace, if your mind were quiet, there would be no need to meditate. An unruly mind doesn't mean that you're not cut out for meditation, it is the very reason you undertake the practice in the first place, the very problem you're trying to remedy."

Peace of Mind

I am about to disclose the secret to peace of mind. Drum roll please.

The secret to peace of mind is very difficult to understand.

It's a good thing I spent all those years in graduate school because this thing is *complex*. If you did not have the good fortune to spend many years in graduate school, I hope you have been keeping up to date with the latest scientific journals. Here goes, the mystery of the ages.

The secret to peace of mind is:

Don't talk, Listen.

I'll repeat:

Don't talk, Listen.

That's it. I was just kidding about the scientific journals.

What does this mean? It means that while you are talking - inwardly, to yourself - you are lost in ego = mind = thinking. You are lost in what Buddhism calls Samsara. While you are talking inwardly, you are obsessing about your dilemma.

The moment you are inwardly still, the moment you enter the state of listening, you are available to something greater, beyond the preoccupations of the ego which is equivalent to the talking itself.

The converse is also true. If you are not peaceful, you are probably in a state of talking. If you are not peaceful, you are probably embroiled in some internal drama that roils the otherwise still waters. If you are not peaceful and wish to be peaceful, abandon whatever story you are embedded in and return to listening, to stillness. Be still. Or as Ramana would often say: Keep quiet.

Combat

Kendra is at war with herself; her mind is the battlefield. Grenades of thought are tossed furiously first in one direction, then another.

Meditation is often associated with relaxation and relaxation is a profound accomplishment, the return to the zero stress state. But meditation may first be more like hand to hand combat: a fierce battle to subdue the raging mind.

In this case the talking/thinking is itself the war. One thought makes one statement, another contradicts and the chaos continues. Keep quiet. To shift into listening is to lay down your weapons. Be still and so choose to be at peace.

The Practice of Listening

Anything can be listened to. I mean listening in the broadest sense, as something done not necessarily with the ears and hearing, but with attention or awareness.

You can listen literally to sound: music, the river flowing, the birds singing, the chorus of crickets, the wind in the trees. The object listened to becomes the anchor for attention. But you can also listen in the broader sense to the information of all the senses: the touch of wind on your cheek, the movement of leaves in the wind, the sunlight sparkling on the leaves, the sunlight sparkling on the water. You can listen to another person - not just when they speak, but to their presence. You can listen to whatever life presents in any moment.

In the more formal sense of meditation, you can listen to breathing. Breathing is a very useful focus for meditation because the breath is always present and in motion. The breath is always available to be listened to. And there is a correlation between breathing and mind - as breathing becomes more regular, mind also tends to subside.

There are many variations on breathing meditation. Previously I talked about watching breathing and labeling thought as "thinking, thinking," as a way of creating distance from the content of thought. Breaths can also be counted, usually on the outbreath, inwardly saying "one" on the first outbreath, "two" on the second, up until ten and then starting over. The counting occupies the verbal mind, gives it a task so that, occupied with the neutral counting, mind is withheld from wandering. The counting also provides an additional focus. You know if you lose count before ten, or if you go beyond ten before realizing that you have lost focus. This technique is very helpful when the mind is haywire and needs a tight leash.

In the section on mantra, we mentioned that the mantra can be coordinated with breathing, recited inwardly usually on the outbreath. Say "peace," for example, inwardly as you breathe out. Or if the mind is fairly quiet, the breathing can be listened to without counting or labeling, without any use of the verbal mind at all.

There are other variations on meditation as listening. You can listen to your heart beating. The heartbeat is very internal and requires that attention becomes quiet in order to hear and feel the quiet heart. Or the body rather than breathing can be the primary object. Systematically moving attention up and down the body, noticing body sensations, is a common and powerful meditation practice. As the body is given attention, knots of tension rise to the surface and release, with a freeing of the energy bound in the knot. The body does not want to stay tight and contracted. The tightness is felt as a painful symptom. Giving deep attention to bodily contractions allows the body to release accumulated tension, and return to the tension free state accompanied by a relief from symptoms.

Thought itself can be a primary object. It is interesting just to observe thoughts popping up. When the mind is busy, this can be useful because the busyness becomes the very thing you attend to. As thoughts pop up, because they are noticed and not entertained, they dissolve immediately.

Listening can be done in its purest form with no focus at all, just listening, just awareness. This was called "choiceless awareness" by J. Krishnamurti. Earlier I suggested a parallel between mastering mind and a musical instrument. Choiceless awareness, like jazz improvisation, is an advanced practice that can only be undertaken once attention is concentrated to the point that no primary object is needed. You are able just to listen, just to be present to life without any technique. This represents the transition into non-dualism, as we will see.

Meditation is necessary because the untrained mind is so erratic that, for practical purposes, some practice of sanity needs to be undertaken - and probably for a very long time - before stillness and simplicity can arise. But let's move forward into non-duality, completing the map we proposed at the outset.

Duality

Meditation requires a cessation of talking in order to listen. Talking is disengaged again and again by returning attention to the primary object. This breaks the habit of thinking. As thinking wanes, there is relief from the tyranny of mind and settling into the present, as one listens to the object of meditation appearing in the present.

There is one problem with the meditation practices I have described. They are dualistic. In other words, there is a subject, "Solomon" (substitute your own name), focusing on something else, an object: sounds, the breath, the body, thoughts or whatever else the primary focus might be. There is always a separation between the subject and object. The subject uses effort to keep attention trained on the object, and this effort creates tension. It also maintains the sense of the subject, in here, looking at something else out there, even if the out-there is within the body, as with breathing. The subject is looking at breathing and everything else. It leaves the subject unexamined. Like the person wearing glasses but looking for his glasses, looking out-there neglects to look at what is most obvious and therefore most concealed: the looker.

As long as "Solomon" remains unexamined he appears to be a discreet entity, and that entity is separate from everything else. There is this core, "Solomon," and everything else is not-Solomon. There is a seemingly unbridgeable gap between myself and everything else. This leaves me uneasy because I am always separate and slightly alienated from a world that is other.

If I am always separate I can never feel entirely complete. I am never at one and at peace in a world that is other. As long as there is a separate entity, how can he be at one with everything he is separate from? There is a gulf between myself and my Beloved, my heart's deepest longing for peace, wholeness, and completion.

Deep Sleep: Perfect Peace

There is, however, a common experiential metaphor for the peace of oneness. When am I completely at peace? In deep sleep, of course. Not dreaming, when the mind is active, but in deep sleep when the mind is silent and I am fully absorbed into myself. There is complete and utter respite, an absence of all conflict.

When I awaken, my story awakens. As soon as waking Consciousness dawns, I pick up the thread of my identity with all its familiar nuances, plots and subplots. When I awaken my problem awakens as well.

Now, is it possible to remain inwardly still even after awakening, so that I retain the peace of sleep in the waking state? In deep sleep I was at peace but I was unconscious. Is it possible to retain that peace while conscious? Yes, if the mind can remain still without picking up the thread of time and identity. Deep sleep is a metaphor for Nirvana.

Startled

Upon being awakened suddenly from a deep sleep,
a sleep taken at some time out of the ordinary,
not the usual nighttime sleep in the familiar bed,
but a midday nap maybe home from work on a snow day,
the phone suddenly rings, you awaken suddenly,
there is a sense of disorientation,
not knowing where you are, when you are, at what point in time,
and it takes a moment for memory to kick in,
to reestablish the story line...
oh yes, I am in the study of my home,
it's afternoon, it's snowing, it's okay, I don't need to be anywhere...
and the remembering is done at first with some urgency,
because for a moment, you know, you had dropped the ball,
the whole ego identity, that whole ball of wax,
that whole burden, perhaps, like Atlas, being shouldered.
But what was retained was essential Being;
that you existed was never in question,
in fact, there was great peace in that sleep,

carried momentarily over to the waking state.
You had withdrawn to the heart of Being,
the obvious and effortless and spontaneous,
and direct sense of yourself,
unburdened by the definitions and conditions of time and space.
Now, can that sense of pure Being,
prior to any concept of where and what you are be held,
for there is peace in Being,
and trouble in the world of conditions?

Prelude

We were just able to identify the title of Emma's movie: "I'm afraid I'm a failure, and I'm afraid they think I'm a failure." This story has been a dominant theme in Emma's life.

I believe every life has a few dominant themes. A few deep questions are asked and a lifetime is spent in working out, to the satisfaction of the soul, the answers to those questions.

Emma received the worst abuse in her family of origin. The abuse created emotional impediments that Emma had to overcome, as if she had weights around her ankles as she pushed off the starting blocks and into adult life. Because of her relatively slow start, having first to recover from the emotional confusion left by the abuse, it seemed to Emma that her siblings were sailing along while she was left behind, not where she ought to be and needing to catch up. Her underlying feeling is: I am not where I should be, and I am afraid the others are judging me for not being as successful; the failure in the family.

Emma asked, what would be a better thought? "I'm doing the best that I can?"

Yes, absolutely. That is a better thought. Instead of a thought that tastes of failure, try one that tastes of forbearance and compassion for self.

But there is an alternative: the Who question. With the Who question, rather than replace a bad thought with a better thought, we look instead for the source of the thought. To whom does this thought arise? Withdraw energy from the story and instead place the energy on: "To whom does the story arise? Who is the knower of the story? Who am I?" The story is then deprived of its energy as attention is directed toward the more fundamental inquiry: From whom does the story arise?

The Who Question

Ramana Maharshi embodied perhaps the most perfect realization of Self ever recorded. His disciple, H.W.L. Poonja, known as Papaji, was a towering master in his own right. I strongly recommend becoming acquainted with their teachings. Central to those teachings is the practice of Self-inquiry which is carried out by asking oneself, "Who am I?" This inquiry is meant to be practiced continuously. When other thoughts arise, rather than follow the other thoughts, one should ask, "To whom do these thoughts arise?" as a way of redirecting attention away from the thoughts and back toward the "Who am I?"

The Who Question is a sword that cuts mind and all illusion off at the root. If thoughts arise, to whom do they arise? If I am troubled, rather than entertain the "I am troubled" thought, who is it that is troubled? If I am depressed, rather than entertain the "I am depressed" thought, who is it that is depressed? If I desire, who desires? If I am frustrated, who is frustrated? Rather than follow the story, any story, to whom does the story arise? Commitment to this practice is the death of the mind. Like a parasite that feeds on its host, mind is deprived of its lifeblood.

The Who Question turns the mind, which is always focused out-there, toward objects and the world, back upon itself. Mind is not now looking outwardly toward objects, but inwardly toward its own source. From where does the mind arise? What precedes the mind?

There is no direct answer to the question, "Who am I?" If an answer appeared that answer would be an object of awareness and we could again say, "To whom does the answer appear?" The answer to the Who question is the stopping of the mind in its tracks and abiding as Being. Being itself is the answer, the mind's stopping is the answer, not an answer the mind can produce. We return home to ourselves, to the simplicity of Being.

For practical purposes, so as to give the mind something to hold to, the answer to the Who question is "I." To whom does the thought arise? To me, to the "I." So simply hold to the feeling of "I." By doing so story and time are negated. "I" - the sense of Being - precedes mind, story, and time. What is left is just I-ness, I Am, the prodigal son home at last, free at last, here and now, Being, the peace of the heart, all signifying the same thing.

The Tree

Ramana Maharshi would say:

What is the mind?
The mind is a bundle of thoughts.

What is the mind's first thought, the root thought?

The first thought, the root thought in the mind is the thought "I." All other thoughts extend from the thought and sensibility of "I," home ground.

Imagine a tree. The center of the tree is the trunk. All the other branches extend from the trunk. The branches are many, dense and complex, but they extend from a single trunk.

The trunk is the sense of "I." All other thoughts extend from "I." The mind, like the canopy of the tree, has many thoughts, much complexity, but all the complexity stems from "I," the simplicity of the knower which precedes the complexity. The complexity is mind losing focus. The return to the sense of "I" is like returning home where all is well, quiet and full. "I" is the name of the heart.

Think about it. All thoughts pertain to you. I feel this. I want this. I like this. I don't like this. All the thoughts are emanations from an inescapable and ever present "I." Yet the "I" itself is unexamined. When you say "I," as you do hundreds of times each day, to what do you refer?

Suffering results from losing touch with this center, climbing out on the limbs of mind and feeling unsteady. The farther out you go, the more unsteady you feel because you are out on a limb of thought, far from the center. Peace comes when retreating from the extremities of mind to the sturdy trunk, the heart, the unfailing sense of "I" that never wavers and where peace resides in the stillness prior to thought.

Let's go back to "talking or listening." To stay in the sense of "I" is to stay at center, that is, the listening mode prior to the arising of talking/mind. Climbing out onto branches of thought occurs when you leave listening, leave the center, and begin the talking.

Happiness had been sought out-there by pursuing desire. But desire never seems to fulfill. There is always another desire waiting. Desire is satiated rather in quiescence, not in temporal objects which can never really satisfy, but in returning to the abiding source from which desire springs.

Oblivion Without the Bottle

Terry has a problem with alcohol but, to her credit, she has been sober for over a year. She used alcohol to deal with the overwhelming stress she felt both at work and at home. Alcohol provided an escape from stress, from life: oblivion. Without alcohol, the stress persists with no way to escape, no way to find oblivion without the bottle. But Terry, that is exactly where spirituality is heading, oblivion without the bottle, a mind perfectly at peace in the midst of life so there is no need to escape at all. Finally: oblivion without the bottle. Lobotomy without the surgery?

Waking From the Dream

Have you ever had this experience? You are dreaming at night and are completely immersed in the dream. Suddenly it occurs to you that the experience might not be real, you might just be dreaming. You try to wake yourself up. The immersion in the dream is effectively over once its reality is questioned. You wake with the realization that what momentarily seemed real was actually just a dream.

Something parallel goes on in the waking state. You go through ordinary life wrapped up in your progress as an ego, with its story unfolding over time. But at some point you might ask, "What's going on here? What's this all about?" Instead of routine immersion in the progression of your story, as with the dream, focus shifts out of the story to the context of the story. Instead of simply focusing on the chessboard of life and what your next move might be, you question the game as a whole.

With the question, "What's going on here?" awakening begins.

But the pull of the mind is powerful. Remember that mind *is* story. In order to awaken from the waking dream, from unconsciousness and habit, attention must be withdrawn from mind, the locus of story. So whenever thoughts (and with thoughts, ego) arise, rather than remaining embedded in the thought, attention is diverted to the

Who question: not the thought, which would only sustain the story, but to whom does the thought arise? The water is diverted from the ancient riverbed through which it has flowed since time immemorial.

So: *interest in finding the source of the story must be greater than interest in the story.* Otherwise you stay involved in the story for lack of genuine interest in awakening. *The desire to awaken must be greater than the desire for the dream.* Otherwise you remain in the dream for the interest you derive as an ego, with its path and dilemma unfolding over time.

The Decision to Divorce

Unfortunately, you cannot fake the commitment to exercise. The commitment must be authentic or you will not drag yourself out of bed early, lace on the running shoes, get yourself to the track, start running, and stay running more days than not.

Unfortunately, you cannot fake the commitment to truth. If the commitment to truth is not authentic, you will continue to entertain thought and story. You will not diligently abandon story in favor of the source of story, mind in favor of the source of mind.

Kelly talked about her decision to divorce her abusive husband. She said, "I was completely fed up. I knew heart and soul that I was done."

Now, Kelly, divorce your mind. The decision to divorce your mind must come from the same depth of feeling: I absolutely do not want this any longer. I am done with mind and illusion. I want to be free.

Illusion is like a mobile that hangs over an infant's crib. It is brightly colored, makes delightful sounds, enchanting. The enchantment with brightly colored illusion must wane and the desire for something more substantial deepen. Only when the commitment to truth is authentic will illusion be forsaken, allowing for the emergence of something greater.

The Non-Dual

We come to the obvious. Previously we talked about the light in the projector shining through the beautiful or not so beautiful images in the film. We talked about pouring the Miracle–Gro™ of attention onto the flowers and not the weeds. With the practice of Self-inquiry, focus is shifted from the object on which the energy is poured to the energy itself. You abide *as* the light; you abide *as* the Miracle–Gro™. All these methods for controlling the mind, the image held before the light, forgetting the most obvious: the light itself.

The Truth of Your Being

I have only met with Jenna twice. She struggles with weight and depression; the two are related. Though she has lost some weight she is still subject to binges. She can eat a package of chocolates in one sitting; the same with chips or ice cream. After doing so, she calls herself a loser and depression kicks in.

She understood me immediately. Jenna, there is no reality to the thought, "I want potato chips," other than the reality you impart. The thought is not real. Ask yourself, "To whom does the thought arise?" and withdraw reality from the thought. Remember: the desire for truth must overcome the desire for illusion, the belief that anything insubstantial and in the realm of time can actually provide abiding happiness.

Desire

Desire is often considered the cause of suffering - referring to the Second Noble Truth of craving - and the fuel that keeps the wheel of birth and death turning. But desire is also the fuel of awakening and creative enterprise, in this sense.

The desire for - shall we say the *commitment* to - awakening must be profound so that other considerations are relinquished. This primary desire keeps secondary desires at bay. And primary desire is also necessary to complete any difficult enterprise. Desire/commitment is the conscious harnessing of intention and focus, and is essential to avoid the dispersion of energy into distraction; the return to ultimately unsatisfying compensations which are, in fact, causes of suffering.

What is Substantial?

What is substantial?
I am vaguely hungry and want to be satisfied.
I think I will try a piece of chocolate.
Umm, the chocolate is tasty but does not go too deep.
I still want something.
So I'll try a square meal.
I'll go to the all—you—can—eat buffet.
Oh, am I stuffed but know that, in a few hours,
I will feel hungry again.
Maybe I should try sex.
Time to sidle up to my wife.
Sex is good but I know that soon I will feel hungry again.

Everything that comes, it seems, goes.
Nothing that comes and goes seems really to satisfy.
What will satisfy my hunger?
Wait, I think I know.
It's obvious: *what does not come and go?*
What is substantial?
I Am.

Reliable

Everything that happens - which is to say *in time* -
everything that comes and goes is unreliable.
Success may or may not come about.
Careers may or may not rise to the desired heights.
Wealth may or may not materialize.
People may or may not end up disappointing.
Friendships may or may not endure.
Intimate relationships may or may not fulfill their promise.
Good times, times of ease, may last or maybe not.
Your own body may or may not remain healthy.
Pain will come and if all goes well it will pass, but maybe not.
Nothing that appears can be relied on, invested in, trusted.
The only thing that can be completely trusted,
is altogether beyond appearance.
If there is no investment, no dependence on anything:
no object, no thought, no feeling, no idea, no opinion,
no hope for better times yet to come,
no relationship, no aspiration, no expectation,
then where does that leave you?
Stay there.
That is always there.
That is God.
That is Self.
That is pure.
That is peace.
That can always be trusted.

Kosher: Ethics

As a child I grew up in a Kosher home. Kosher means clean. In a Kosher home, in compliance with Jewish dietary laws originating in the Hebrew Bible, certain foods are considered pure and may be eaten, and other foods are considered impure and are not to be consumed. The dietary laws were an evolutionary step forward in their day. The laws of "Kashrut" - the "Kosher" laws - mostly describe which meat and fish is Kosher and permitted, and which meat and fish is considered impure. I have a gone a step further and am now a vegetarian so, in my present version of dietary laws, no meat and fish should be consumed on ethical grounds.

It amazes me that people will eat almost anything. Any creature - however conscious and evolved, however primitive and slimy - can be killed and eaten to satisfy one's curiosity and appetite.

Learning as a child to keep Kosher was very useful. It taught me that certain behaviors are strictly off limits, impure, and that behavior needs to be disciplined. There is a line of purity that should not be crossed.

If overweight is an issue, chips and chocolate should be considered off limits, not Kosher, beyond the line of purity that should not be crossed.

The idea of restraint from the impure extends beyond food to all behavior, establishing the principles of ethics. In Buddhism, for example, similar to the Ten Commandments, the path to the end of suffering begins with Five Precepts which establish guidelines for right behavior. The Five Precepts are:

1. Refrain from killing *any* creature. This precept can be extended to refrain from any form of violence.

2. Refrain from stealing. Do not take what you are not entitled to. I extend this precept to include one's overall relationship to materiality and money. Try to avoid dealing with money in ways that will create anxiety. Try not to overextend financially.

3. Refrain from inappropriate sexual behavior. Joseph Goldstein, one of my first teachers, defined this as sexual behavior that causes suffering for oneself or others.

4. Refrain from lying or other forms of wrong, crude or abusive speech.

5. Refrain from the use or abuse of alcohol and other intoxicants. Alcohol and drugs are terribly overused in our culture. Alcohol tends to unbalance the mind and to numb its capacity for subtle perception.

These precepts are guidelines; crossing them, like crossing the double yellow line in the road, is risky and done at one's peril. The precepts define five very powerful areas of life that require great care: killing and violence, stealing and materiality, sexuality, speech, and intoxicants. But the precepts are not written in stone. Lawrence Kohlberg developed stages of moral reasoning, and it is conceivable that the precepts may be broken, the double yellow line appropriately and wisely crossed, as an expression of the highest stage of moral reasoning. If a drunk driver is coming at you head on, by all means cross the double yellow line and get out of the way! An often asked hypothetical question is: If you were in a room with Hitler in 1938, knowing that over fifty million people would die during the coming war, would you pull the trigger? Of course! Hypothetical questions are not really useful because in reality one responds to situations spontaneously. I mention this just to illustrate that even killing may be a moral action in certain situations. And mosquitoes in summer? Well, they don't stand much chance.

At first these restrictions are upheld in conformance to the authority of the teaching, like following directions on faith, trusting that the directions are sound. But as the mind become subtler its tastes organically change, and behavior that stems from an impure state of mind, impure food and entertainments naturally lose their appeal. Violence ceases to be entertaining.

Continuing the progression, at subtler levels, negative *thoughts* are immediately felt as impure, distasteful, and are eschewed. Even further, *all* unnecessary thought begins to feel impure, noisy, unwelcome static. The line of discernment is redrawn to exclude subtler forms of illusion which inherently lose their appeal.

In the Hebrew Bible, it is told that Moses in the desert was instructed by God to speak to a rock, and water would flow for the thirsty Israelites. But Moses erred and struck the rock instead. The water flowed but for this error, for this deviation from the divine will, Moses was forbidden to enter the Promised Land. As Consciousness evolves, error becomes ever more subtle, the line of purity and illusion ever more refined.

Havdallah

Hamavdil ben kodesh l'chol...
"He who separates between the sacred and the prosaic."
This Hebrew prayer ends the Sabbath,
and ushers in the new week of worldly activity.
But the idea is much wider.
The distinction between the sacred and the prosaic,
must be made perpetually;
no harbor given to prosaic thoughts,
no invitation to the drama of Samsara given at all.
Rather, when there is a perpetual renunciation of the prosaic,
a perpetual cognizance of the sacred remains.

Case Study

Cara had an ah-hah moment. She realized that through life she has had a defeatist attitude. The attitude was programmed early on: "Why can't you be more like your brother." She bought into the suggestion that she was insufficient, the suggestion "took" and, without realizing it, she has gone through life with the unconscious mantra: "You just know you're not going to succeed."

But now the programming has become conscious. She sees it now. The question becomes: how to deal with this negative mantra that has been so much a part of her identity.

I reminded her that the creative light - I am - is, like film in a projector, shining through the image of insufficiency that she holds in mind. The subject - I am - has attached itself to the predicate - a loser. Her mantra, without realizing it, has been "I am a loser" (You know you're not going to succeed, Cara. You know in the end you will screw it up. You know things never work out for you); a formula for unhappiness.

So anytime that thought comes up - and it will because it is well established in the mental landscape - she must play defense: disinvest, withdraw reality from the thought. To whom does the thought arise? Return to the radiance of Being that lends apparent reality to the thought which will wither from lack of sustenance.

Or using methods from Positive-thinking, go on the offense. Take the thought "I am Blessed by God," and hold to it. Pour the Miracle-Gro^{TM} of attention there, sow this new seed in the inner landscape, retrain the muscle memory of mind, and so align more closely with joy.

Russian Dolls

Last Mother's Day, at the craft fair on the town common, I bought Russian dolls for my wife. Beautifully painted, blue filigree on white, ten dolls, one inside the other. The outermost doll is quite large and the tenth doll in is quite tiny.

We are constructed in layers something like Russian dolls. The outermost doll is the largest, most inclusive doll, the doll that contains all the other dolls. After the largest doll, there are dolls at one level, then another level of remove from the largest, most inclusive doll.

The largest, most inclusive doll in the way we are constructed is Consciousness. Everything is contained within Consciousness, so Consciousness can be said to be our most fundamental nature. This is like saying, while there are many characters and plots in a movie, the most fundamental aspect of the movie is the light. No light, no movie. Consciousness is the light that brings life and all its contents into Being.

Consciousness and Being are synonymous. To Be is to be Conscious. Your existence, from your point of view, is not conceivable apart from your being Conscious. If there were no Consciousness, you would not know that you existed. If it could be proposed that you could exist without Consciousness, still, your existence wouldn't do you any good; subjectively it would be a non-event. You would be lights out, inert like a rock (I don't mean to disparage the rock, which may also be Conscious at some atomic level). So Consciousness is the same thing as Being, just as the existence of a movie is inconceivable apart from the light. Consciousness and Being are the same thing.

Let's go back to the Heart and the All. As I approach the heart, as I approach the most central aspect of my Being, I transcend all the more limited ideas, labels, and notions that I have about myself. This is like saying that, as I approach the heart of the movie, I approach the light beyond all the specifics of the movie. As I approach my heart, I am also increasingly without definition. "I Am;" that is all. Light; that is all. So, "I Am" is the most central and obvious condition of my existence, and within this "I Am" the world appears. By approaching the most central aspect, and eschewing the more limited ideas I have about myself, I also approach the largest, most inclusive aspect of my Being. And here is where the Russian Doll metaphor breaks down; as you get closer in, you also get farther out. The Heart and the All are the same thing. So let's reverse the metaphor for a moment. Rather than approach from the perspective of the All, let's approach from the perspective of the Heart.

There is a coffee cup on the table. I can observe the coffee cup. I do not think that I am the coffee cup. The coffee cup is outside of "me." But I can also observe my thoughts. I can observe my thoughts just as I observe the coffee cup. In this sense, thoughts are outside of "me." Like rings in a bull's eye, "I," the heart, is more central than the thoughts which are one ring out. Thoughts, mind, are at one level of remove from "me."

Papaji uses sleep as a metaphor. When I am in deep sleep I am in a very central place. I am "all the way in." I am aware of neither mind nor body. When I start to dream, however, mind awakens. While dreaming I am one ring out, aware of mind but not of body.

It can be said that Consciousness is comparable to deep sleep, ground zero, home, all the way in. Mind is at one level of remove from Consciousness, just as dreaming is at one level of remove from deep sleep. Mind is contained within Consciousness.

After dreaming I awaken more fully outward and become aware of my body. Then I fully awaken outward and perceive the world. It could be said, then, that Consciousness is most central, mind is at one level of remove, then body, then world.

The Russian doll metaphor is useful to convey the sense of layers, especially the idea that *mind is not Self,* but is *known by* Self and so is at one level of remove from most intimate Self which is Consciousness or Being. But it can also be said that there are no layers whatsoever. Everything is contained in Consciousness. Everything is lit up by

Consciousness. All the apparently different images in the movie are really all made up of the light that animates the movie.

So it can be said that all is Consciousness. All the seemingly separate objects in the movie - the house, the table, the cat - appear within Consciousness and are not other than Consciousness. There is only a "movie" of seemingly separate objects but the entire "movie" is really seamless, undifferentiated light. In this sense, everything I experience is light, Consciousness. The mind and body, no less than the house or the cat, all appear within the light of Consciousness and so are not other than that light. *All I have ever known or experienced is Consciousness. All anyone has ever, could ever, or will ever know is Consciousness. Knowing* is *Consciousness.*

A Shift in Perspective

Do you remember this picture from your textbooks in school? The picture looked like a chalice at first, but if you shifted perspective you saw not a chalice but two faces looking at each other? Nothing changed, just a shift in perspective.

Ramana would ask: Are you in the world or is the world in you?

From the conventional perspective, I am in the world. "Solomon" is an entity, a mind/body in a greater entity, the world. From this perspective, Solomon is a tiny body contained in a very large universe.

But with a shift in perspective I find that all experience - the world - appears within Consciousness. Everything is contained in the largest Russian Doll of Consciousness. In this sense the world is in me. Everything I experience or have ever experienced is within my Knowing. The world arises and has always arisen within Knowing. And the same is true for everyone else: everything that has ever been Known has arisen within Knowing.

The Majesty Within

A popular self-help book is entitled: Don't Sweat the Small Stuff… and It's All Small Stuff (Carlson, 1996). I thought of calling this book: *The Majesty Within… and It's All Within.*

"The Majesty Within," is an image that came during meditation. It seemed to describe the meditative state when the mind is still and the heart is open: the majesty of the inner world.

But there is a second meaning to the phrase. As Ramana says, I am not in the world, the world is in me. From the perspective of the largest doll of Consciousness, the majesty of the outer world - the entire pageant of life - is also within Consciousness. *There is no without.* There is no duality, no two-ness, no within and without. What appears to be outside the body is still *within* Consciousness. So the seeming "outer" world in all its glory - earth, trees, lakes, rivers, people, cities, sky, stars - is also the majesty within, taking myself as Being/Consciousness within which everything appears. The majesty of the inner and outer worlds; there is no demarcation. Everything is equally the majesty within unboundaried Being. The world is in me.

If there is no without then there also can be no external God. God cannot be an object of experience. If you were to go to heaven and see

God, then God, like all other objects of experience, would still appear within You. You, as Consciousness, remain the unchanging context within which this appearance of God appears. Further, God would be something that becomes present but which was not always present, so this appearance of God - which comes and goes - cannot be God. God cannot be a temporary appearance or experience. God - the intimation of spirit, love, beauty, meaning, intelligence, majesty - is the ever present intimation of your own essence, the spirit that you are and have always been. You are that spirit; it is and cannot be outer and other.

The Light of Being

Conventional consciousness is the consciousness, "I am in the world." From this perspective, I am a body/mind in a world that is other. This is the dualistic perspective. There is me, the subject, and the rest of the world is other than me, objects appearing to my subjectivity. Subject-object; duality; separation. My center of gravity as a subject is a body/mind. I take myself to be an ego, a separate being.

But from the perspective of Russian Dolls, there is a larger context within which the body/mind appears. This context is Consciousness. The body/mind that I take myself to be appears within Consciousness, and so this Consciousness is more fundamentally my nature, more the truth of what I am. Solomon and the rest of the world appear in the movie that is illuminated by the light of Being. Solomon and his entire story requires the light of Being to *Be*.

As my center of gravity shifts from being a body/mind in the world, to being the Consciousness within which the body/mind and the world arises, as my center of gravity shifts toward context, toward ground rather than figure, I no longer see myself as Solomon in the world but, rather, Solomon and his world appears in Consciousness. I am Consciousness, the light of Being within which the body/mind and world appear.

So my deeper nature is the light of Being that animates the movie of the world. At night, in deep sleep, the world disappears but I continue to exist, unchanged, whether or not there is a movie. The appearance or non-appearance of a movie does not impact the fact of my existence. At night, in deep sleep, I exist but for a time no movie is playing. As Nisargadatta has said, in sleep I am aware that I am unaware. I am aware of darkness. I remain Consciousness, I continue to exist, but the movie that is playing is darkness.

The taste of freedom is the realization that you are the light of Being. You are not defined by the body/mind or any story. All of that appears within your deeper nature as the light, but the light is not affected by the movie.

Your job is to remain as the light, the Consciousness within which the movie of life appears. Actually it is impossible not to be the light, but sometimes we mistake ourselves to be the body/mind. As a body/mind there is the possibility of suffering when desires are frustrated. But if you remain as the light, there is no demand on the movie. There is no demand that the movie turn out one way or another.

It could be said that the light is perfect. The movie, then, is always perfect as an expression of the perfect light, not because the movie turns out perfectly, according to my desire. Therefore this moment, and every moment, without mind and its stories suggesting otherwise, is perfect. Again the title of the book by Sailor Bob Adamson: "What's Wrong with Right Now, Unless You Think About It." Here is the possibility of a perfection inherent in Being/Consciousness, in life itself, without the requirement that the movie be a particular way, according to my desire.

Yugas

We go through life trying to line up the chess pieces just right, but doing so is difficult. Something is always not quite to our liking. Health may not be perfect. Finances may not be perfect. Relationships may not be perfect.

Even if the pieces line up in my own life, they may not in my extended life. Others in my family may be ill or suffering. Their lives may not be lined up. Or if my immediate family is doing well, there may be trouble among friends, the more extended family, and in the human family some crisis always prevails. Whether close to home or in the larger human family, some crisis always prevails. Perfection in circumstances is elusive.

The millennial aspiration is for the kingdom of heaven on earth, perfect circumstances. I suppose this may come to pass at some point. Indian thought contains the notion of Yugas, ascending and descending ages of light and darkness. Golden ages yield to silver, bronze and iron ages, and the cycle re-ascends over enormous stretches of time. According to this philosophy we are presently in a dark age, a Kali Yuga; divine harmony is not readily apparent in the life of the world.

There is merit in being in a dark age. It affords the opportunity to grow through working out darkness, individually and collectively. In the spiritual iron age, we hammer out truth in the forge of suffering.

But in trying to find the right formula for the individual and collective economies, for human relations, the environment and so on, focus remains on arranging the chess pieces correctly. In doing so, it is easy to overlook a perfection that is true independent of circumstances, the only perfection really possible since perfection in circumstances is elusive.

In speaking with someone recently about meditation, I suggested she find the place within herself that is pre-aggravation. The mind always has a problem, a project, something that needs doing before perfection is attained. That being so, there will be an eternity of projects to complete before a golden age of perfect circumstances can occur.

Everyone is walking around obsessing about their dilemmas. I am inclined to say, "Be still. Recognize an imminent perfection rather than perfection in the future once all your projects are completed. Perfection and the taste of eternity is present now." There will always be another project and perfection will never arrive or, if it does momentarily, before the cycle inevitably descends.

To be present is to acknowledge perfection in the light of Being, in Consciousness, in life itself. It is to look to one's own source, the substratum of all-that-is for happiness. It is not to have a grocery list of things that need to be accomplished before happiness can be present. It is to derive joy from the miracle and beauty that is always *here*.

The attempt to get everything right - to lose the weight, pad the bankbook - is to have a project and thus to overlook imminence. Imminence is always true and so deriving happiness from imminence is always available. All that is needed is to withdraw attention from mind and its projects, from obsessing within time, from happiness in the future, to settle into the I Am and see wonder.

Equanimity

You know how you can adjust the speed at which the computer mouse moves the cursor? If the speed is set to the maximum, a slight movement of the mouse will send the cursor careening across the screen. The sensitivity is set too high and needs to be turned down. This is also the case when the mind reacts with too much sensitivity to the environment. An offhand remark, a stray glance, or a cloudy day; a very slight stimulus and the mind reels in disarray.

Let's say mood is very sensitive to weather. I feel fine today because it is sunny and 80. Tomorrow though (this is spring in New England, after all) it will be cloudy and 50, and I will hang my head. If mood is too sensitive to external stimuli, wellness is always fragile.

If wellness comes from within, however, if the mind is stable and not subject to the vagaries of fortune, then wellness is not fragile at all. You have solved your problem. You are firmly established in peace and can be a beacon to others, a reminder that light is always the case and available within, beneath the clamoring of mind.

$24 million

I am visiting an old friend in Washington, DC. Last night we went to the ballpark to see a game, Red Sox - Nationals. The Nationals won 9-3 behind great pitching. It was the largest crowd ever to attend a game at Nationals Park thanks to the Red Sox. Probably more Boston fans than home grown in the stands.

At the game, my friend said that his colleague is related to the family that sold the Red Sox to its new ownership and that his colleague's share of the sale was $24 million. Wow, big numbers!

As this is being written, I am still in DC, in a park across the street from the White House, sitting under a shade tree. It is a pleasant spot on a pleasant day.

There is an inclination to think, "I wish I had $24 million." But what would be that different? I am sitting in a lovely spot, in a lovely place, watching the movements of interesting people, laptop in hand, writing. What is insufficient? If I had $24 million in the bank would my experience sitting in this park in this moment be very different?

I grabbed a book by Ramana Maharshi for the trip.* It says: "Liberation is our very nature. We are that. The very fact that we wish for liberation shows that freedom from all bondage is our real nature."

The $24 million would seem to bestow that very sense of *freedom from all bondage*. Twenty four million dollars would allow every opportunity to pursue every dream and desire. Even so there will always be limitations of one sort or another. I do not have wings to fly.

But what bondage do I experience at this very moment? What could be deemed insufficient? Only the bondage inherent in mind itself. Only the insufficiency in mind's complaint with life.

Bondage is not the inability to own a yacht or a baseball team or to flap my wings and fly. There will always be *some* external limitation. Bondage is in being here, always here, and feeling ill at ease, wishing I were somewhere else or had something else. Craving.

Say I have $24 million and sail the world on a yacht. Would my state of mind on that yacht be substantially different from the present state of mind, sitting in a park, under a pleasant shade tree, opposite the White House?

The same book says: "If a man thinks that his happiness is due to external causes and his possessions, it is reasonable to conclude that his happiness must increase with the increase of possessions and diminish in proportion to their diminution. Therefore if he is devoid of possessions, his happiness should be nil. What is the real experience of man? Does it conform to this view?

In deep sleep man is devoid of possessions, including his own body. Instead of being unhappy he is quite happy. Everyone desires to sleep soundly. The conclusion is that happiness is inherent in man and is not due to external causes. One must realize the Self in order to open the store of unalloyed happiness."*

The sense of desire, of being on this park bench or wherever you may be, and feeling it to be insufficient is the real problem. Disturbance of mind is the real problem. At night, in deep sleep, in the absence of disturbance, there is perfect peace and you have gained nothing. Perfection is a state of mind, the absence of craving, the abandonment of the ego, and is not dependent on circumstances.

So, if one is able to *silence* desire, as in deep sleep, to settle into the heart and allow its peace, its completeness, there is a joy that requires nothing. One is able to sit on a park bench, or wherever you may be, without taking yourself to be anything in particular, to be free of story, including the story, "Boy, I wish I had $24 million." I am the glow of and delight in Being and its manifestations. I am free from any thought of lack, of needing something different or more, for everything that arises, arises within the unchanging. For this you do not need $24 million.

*Godman, David. Be As You Are: The Teachings of Sri Ramana Maharshi. P.13, P.16.

Money

Money is material freedom. The more money I have, the freer I am to pursue the fulfillment of material desire, to move the pieces on the chessboard of life, to create the heaven of my imagining.

Happiness is generally sought by pursuing perfection in outer circumstances. The more money I have, the better able I am to approach the perfection of circumstances and so to be happy.

Money is wonderful. Money is freedom of a kind, nothing less, not to be denigrated. With money, I can help not only myself but many others relieve material suffering and acquire greater freedom.

If I have money, if I so desire, I can live in the heart of the city, at the most fashionable address, dine in splendor, while escaping at will to a more countrified setting of warm breezes and beautiful sunsets. Nor do I have to trudge away at the office, working late at night, my desk piled high with papers. I can create pleasure and avoid displeasure.

Even so money cannot create all perfect circumstances. My relationships still may not be successful, and my children's lives are beyond my control. I will still be subject to old age, disease, and death, which no money can avert. And even with vast resources and material blessings, I may not be psychologically free. We all know people with money whose problems money has not solved.

With or without money, everyone is trying to improve outer circumstances, to get to a better place in life. Happiness is generally sought out there, in the future when I resolve my dilemma, when I get things just right.

Psychological freedom, as opposed to the material freedom that money brings, is freedom from craving. It is to be inwardly at peace, to find happiness through the perfection of inner rather than outer circumstances. If I am at peace, if I have dismantled my buttons, if the ego has atrophied with the waning of thought then, like a turtle its shell, I carry this peace with me wherever I go. I am still free to pursue, but do not require perfect outer circumstances, because the state of mind that I was seeking by perfecting outer circumstances, I have found within.

Psychological freedom means that I am at peace whatever my outer circumstances happen to be. Peace, beauty, and not craving is the lens through which life is viewed.

The Broadway Lights

In my early twenties, I lived for a while in a spiritual community in New York City. I worked as a cab driver, nights, in Manhattan, as a way to earn money for living expenses, without being committed to a real job which held no interest at the time.

Late one night, I was driving through the theater district and was flagged by a single man. I recognized him as soon as he got into the cab. He was starring on Broadway and was on his way home to Central Park West, having just completed that night's performance. Before getting this role in the Broadway theater, he was the male lead in one of the most popular TV shows of the day.

I asked him what life was like as a famous and wealthy actor. He was quite open in response. He said that he took up acting because he was a shy person. He hoped that if he became famous, he would be known and sought out socially. At parties, he would not be the unknown guy in the corner, having to explain or justify himself. He would be approached with familiarity and admiration. But fame and wealth, while nice, did not hold the redemption he hoped for. I sensed the doubts that originally moved him toward acting had not altogether healed.

I am on my way home to Massachusetts from DC. In the Metro to the airport, a poster for a self help book was prominently displayed. The book promised, as many do, that your life can fulfill all your dreams. Funny, but the actor came to mind though I hadn't thought of him in years. He was quite famous and wealthy, had fulfilled his dreams, but something was missing.

My flight is delayed. I've got time to spend in the airport terminal. The overhead TV is reporting on all the celebrity deaths this week. Ed McMahon, Farrah Fawcett, Michael Jackson. I do not sense that any of these phenomenally successful people were particularly happy. Yes, they each reached great peaks of success but the peak in each life, as is often the case, was followed by times of great trial.

Most self help advice is about the future. How to become a TV or Broadway star, how to become famous and wealthy, living the life or your dreams, in the future. But you may attain great peaks and, without wisdom, something will be missing, you will continue to look to the future for things finally to be complete.

I suggest searching for a happiness that has no conditions, a happiness that is not in the future, that is eternal and therefore always present, present in the crowded Metro, present in the airline terminal, present now, present as you hold this book, a happiness that is the nature of Being itself, when the mind and ego have been resolved, that does not require the Broadway lights to be.

All God, All the Time

There is only God: All God, All the Time. There is nothing that is not God. Or substitute any of the synonyms for God. There is only Consciousness, there is nothing that is not Consciousness. There is only the Ocean; it is impossible not to be in the Ocean.

This means that, at this moment, at any moment, whatever is happening, whatever is being experienced, including the seeming experiencer, that is God. There is only the Ocean, there is nothing outside the Ocean, the totality.

Problems come only when a thought/story arises. The thought/story is a blip on the radar screen of Consciousness and, if not taken seriously, it instantly vanishes. But if the thought/story is taken seriously, there is involvement in the story, the figure, and a forgetting of the context from which the story arose, the ground. Through involvement in a particular story there is then an illusion, an impression of a separate self, the ego who speaks the story in his or her own voice, and an entering into story, time, dilemma, and suffering. Suddenly the vast horizon is obscured by this little drama of the ego, held just before your eyes, that takes center stage and Samsara is born.

The remedy? To whom does the thought arise? Return to I, to Being, to Self. Acknowledge Divinity. There is only God and its taste, absent mind and dilemma, is peace and happiness.

For practical purposes, when mind begins to run, use whatever technique is appropriate to subdue the running. Return either to a positive thought or to stillness. This may require a use of one method or another along the spectrum. If life seems burdensome, perhaps contemplate things in a way that changes the internal perspective - take a more rational, balanced view; use an affirmation to anchor thinking in a positive focus; or meditate by entering the state of listening to breath or body. Focusing intensely on the body will allow accumulated tensions to release. Anchor attention in a mantra - Acknowledge Divinity - Perfection - or, when mind is subtle and the running has slowed, return to inactivity, the mere sense of I. Use whatever technique works to abandon the thought/story. Either use mind to good effect or relinquish mind altogether.

Remember that mastery of mind is like mastering a musical instrument. It does not come easily. Mastery requires continuous practice. Practice is the commitment to wake from the dream of the ego, to withdraw from the ego's fixation of the moment, the dilemma du jour.

Many spiritual philosophies propose that the pristine soul is encased in samskaras: impressions, the residue of undigested experience that is left from this or former lives. The residue of prior experience amounts to the conditioned mind; the conditioned mind and its patterns is simply the momentum from the past, the movement of a wheel that was once set in motion and is still turning. The essence of spiritual practice is to allow the momentum of the wheel to spin down without adding further momentum to the spinning.

If one is attentively present, no further residue is created. Experience is digested as it happens. No further momentum is added and, eventually, the residual momentum of the wheel slows to a halt. The busyness ends and mind capitulates. The soul balances its accounts and radiant life remains.

Flash Quiz: New Math

Congratulations! We are about to learn the New Math. There is an altogether new equation to learn. Here it is.

Consciousness = Being = God = I Am = Self = Eternity = Bliss

Just as mind=ego=suffering in Math Level I, the context within which mind and everything else arises is Consciousness. From the perspective of Consciousness there is no separation, there is only Being, call it God, Nirvana, Self and its nature is Bliss.

Submerged

When I was twenty years old and visiting home from college, I awoke my mother one night and told her that we needed to go to the Emergency Room. We drove there hurriedly. It turned out I had appendicitis and would need to have surgery the next day. In those days an appendectomy was a major surgical procedure and an incision several inches long was made in my lower abdomen. I remember staying in the hospital for a week. My how times have changed! Now I would be home in a day.

I remember being in the recovery room. I had been under general anesthesia during the procedure, was now vaguely stirring, but was still deeply sedated. I remember hearing a moaning far, far in the distance. I eventually realized that I was producing the sound. But when first stirring, I was so interior that the moaning seemed far away. I was not producing the sound, someone or something else was producing the sound; it was an exterior sound. The sound and the body itself seemed very far from where I was located, deep in my interior, as if I were far below the surface of the ocean and saw a glimmer of light on the surface, but I remained submerged.

In meditation it is possible to feel this same sense of being submerged into the most central but also most comfortable, home-like part of your Being. And from the vantage of being submerged, the world and all its expressions, the world and its accouterments seems endearing, *quaint*. The entire universe seems like a quaint notion far away on the surface. And in this notion of a distant world are all the ideas that you might have about it: ideas of yourself as having a body, ideas of yourself as having a history, the notion of a calendar and years that pass, the notion of a country, the notion of a universe itself all seems distant and fanciful from the vantage of being submerged.

The Size of Being

How big are you?

    A. Five feet

    B. Six feet

C. Seven feet

D. I have no beginning and no end.

In advertisements, sometimes a quarter is placed alongside another object to convey the size of the object relative to the quarter. We know how big a quarter is - it serves as a fixed reference - so we can sense the size of the other object compared to the quarter. But, regarding Consciousness, there is no absolute object, no fixed reference against which to measure. There is no quarter with which to measure the size of Consciousness because any possible object, any fixed reference appears *within* Consciousness. So any idea you have about *your* actual size is just that: an idea. Are you the size of your body? No, your body is an appearance *within* Consciousness. Is your Being the age of your body? No, there is no way to state the age of your Being. There is no "absolute quarter" to say you - as Being - are big or small, young or old, here or there. What you take yourself to be - a body in time and space - is purely conceptual. Better to say: I have no boundary and no sense of ever having been born.

The correct multiple choice answer is D.

Consciousness has no boundaries. Being has no boundaries. All ideas used to define or circumscribe Being are just that: ideas, concepts. Take the concept of time. We call this the year 2013. But that number is just a convenience; it has no real validity. Truer to say we are in a boundless ocean, we are in an eternity that has no demarcations, no beginning or end, and the concept of 2013 is a convenience, relatively but not ultimately useful. Or the concept of place. It might be useful to say that this is Massachusetts, but Massachusetts is a concept, a line on the map, an idea that serves a purpose but which has no real validity; there is no line on the earth with Massachusetts scrawled on one side and New Hampshire on the other. Or your name: a concept used to define your being, but your Being has no boundary, no edge where it begins and ends.

Peace

A breath is born and dies;
it rises and falls within my Being, but I Am not moved.
A day is born and dies;
it rises and falls within my Being, but I Am not moved.
A lifetime is born and dies;
it rises and falls within my Being, but I Am not moved.
A universe is born and dies;
it rises and falls within my Being, but I Am not moved.
I Am at Peace.

Endlessness

If you want the kingdom of heaven you can have it here and now by dropping every idea and concept in your mind. (Godman, David. Nothing Ever Happened, V2. P 166).

The body, the mind, the town in which you live, your name, your story, the United States of America, the year 2013 or whatever number is printed on your calendar, the history of civilization, the planet Earth, the evolution of stars, Time - all are just ideas, just appearances in Endlessness.

As contemplation proceeds, these are all seen to be fanciful notions in a context without beginning or end. You are the context and the appearances within it. All appears, persists, and disappears within your Being, does it not?

Endlessness is endless. There is no end to it. It is inexhaustible. It cannot be exhausted. Beyond the concepts in which you are embedded, that circumscribe your identity, Endlessness is the truer truth of your Being. Your deeper Self is and thus you are Endless.

CHAPTER VI:

ORIGINAL
CONSCIOUSNESS

The map that was proposed at the outset is now complete. We have arrived where No-thinking takes us. We will now consider the implications of Endlessness and its perceiver: Original Consciousness.

Tantra

From an old "Deck House" catalogue, describing the use of passive solar heating in the design of their homes:

"The winter sun shines directly into a broad expanse of sloped, south-facing windows. The sunlight (short-wave radiation) passes through the glass and becomes long-wave radiation (heat) when it touches a solid object inside. At least one of the objects (inside) is a thermal mass, such as a tile floor or a brick wall, which initially stores the heat then radiates it into the house."

Sometimes, when my heart is open, I feel a love without object.
I feel that I carry my love within.
Love is not dependent on external circumstances being just so,
it is rather my essence, my own unalterable nature.
Though I may already feel this love, still, I yearn for my lover.
I want to share my love, to radiate like short-wave radiation,
that becomes heat only when it meets an object.
I miss my lover because my love is deeper,
more complete, more concrete, more palpable, more sensual,
when it shines on her face and her face warms in return.

In this I feel there is an analogue for creation.
I feel I understand why God created the creation.
For though He was complete already in his own love-nature,
still, the creation gave Him the solarium,
the matter, the tile floor, the brick wall,
to transform the radiance of His nature into heat,
to realize His love more fully.

This suggests that God's perfection includes the creation,
and offers an answer to philosophers who ask,
"If God is perfect, why would God need to create the world?"
Yes, but God's perfection includes the world:
a charming complement toward the fullness of love.

Lover and Beloved

This short passage by Meher Baba offers one beautiful and succinct explanation for the existence of the universe:

"God is Love. And Love must love. And to love there must be a Beloved. But since God is Existence infinite and eternal there is no one for Him to love but Himself. And in order to love Himself He must imagine Himself as the Beloved whom He as the Lover imagines He loves.

Beloved and Lover implies separation. And separation creates long-ing; and longing causes search. And the wider and the more intense the search the greater the separation and the more terrible the longing.

When longing is most intense separation is complete, and the purpose of separation, which was that Love might experience itself as Lover and Beloved, is fulfilled; and union follows. And when union is attained, the Lover know that he himself was all along the Beloved whom he loved and desired union with; and that all the impossible sit-uations that he overcame were obstacles which he himself had placed in the path to himself.

To attain union is so impossibly difficult because it is impossible to become what you already are! Union is nothing other than knowl-edge of oneself as the Only One." (Baba, Meher. The Everything and the Nothing. P. 1).

The Meaning of Life

"Union is nothing other than knowledge of oneself as the Only One." Meher Baba is suggesting that I will eventually come to realize that I am the Only One dreaming a dream in which I imagine that I am separate and other than my Self.

This point of view has been maintained by many spiritual masters. Nisargadatta has said, "The words he gave me touched me very deeply. I abided in one thing only: the words of my Guru are the truth, and he said, 'You are the Parabrahman (the Supreme, the Absolute).'" (Dunn, Jean. Prior to Consciousness. P. 1).

Or from a dialogue with Ramana:

Q: I am from God. Is God not distinct from me?

A: Who asks this question? God does not ask it. You ask it. So find who you are and then you may find if God is distinct from you.

Q: But God is perfect and I am imperfect. How can I ever know Him fully?

A: God does not say so. The question is for you. After finding who you are, you may see what God is. (Talks with Ramana Maharshi. P. 458).

Or Papaji:

I always like it when someone stand up and proclaims with authority, "I am God." A man who knows who he really is can stand up and proclaim this truth, because it is his own inner experience, but when people behave like this in the West, they get into trouble both with the Church and with the civil authorities. Anyone who persistently proclaims that he has understood that he is identical with God runs the risk of being put in a mental hospital. (Godman, David. Nothing Ever Happened, V2. P. 198).

Like a thriller with one plot twist after another and a shocking, wholly unexpected ending, the universe holds the ultimate plot twist: You are - this is - Original Consciousness.

Let's go back to Russian Dolls. Usually I take myself to be this rather tiny doll of a body. But in contemplation I recognize that this body appears *to* me, so there is a *me* larger than the body. The body appears within a larger context, as does mind. I see that I am built in layers and keep dis-identifying with the less inclusive layers. I come to see that everything that appears - body, mind, world - appears within unboundaried Consciousness. Anything that is tasted as experience is tasted within a context. That context is the largest, most inclusive of the Russian Dolls: Original Consciousness.

There is good and bad news in this. Let's start with the bad news. In Meher Baba's language, the universe is God imagining that he is not God and seeking Himself. So absent Self-realization the mystery remains unsolved. Absent the realization of Oneness, it will always feel as if something is missing. And Oneness requires the disappearance of the ego, the sense of a separate self: mind.

At the outset we talked about the Buddha's Four Noble Truths which state that the end of suffering is Nirvana. The Eastern masters are making the same statement. You will feel whole only when you fully realize your true nature as Original Consciousness.

There is provisional happiness along the way, certainly. There is happiness in the fulfillment of deeply held desires and in positive states of mind, certainly. But only when Oneness is attained - in Meher Baba's language of love - only when the Self is realized - in Ramana's language of wisdom - only in Nirvana is the purpose of life truly fulfilled, the purpose for which the universe has come into being. Absent this something will always feel incomplete, and any teaching that soft pedals this truth is misleading.

Now to the good news. In Meher Baba's language, God is only imagining that He is separate from Himself. There is no separation.

You are never separate from your Self; how could you be? You are never outside of or other than the ocean of Being, and the form of the body/mind is a bubbling up from the ocean. But mind asserts the separate reality of the bubble, the wave taking itself as independent of the ocean, the acceptance of the chicken thought: I am a body/mind. There is only the bad habit of the ego asserting its separate existence in every thought spoken in the ego's own voice. The illusion of the ego has to be seen through and spiritual practices are all directed toward this end.

From a devotional point of view, as with Meher Baba's path of love, the Beloved must be remembered at all times. The passion for the Beloved becomes so all consuming that everything else is forgotten. The desire for ecstasy of union with the Beloved overcomes all other desires or concerns. Only the Beloved. The lover forgets himself and merges in the Beloved.

From the point of view of wisdom, the desire for Truth must overcome all other desires or concerns. Who Am I? All thoughts are subordinated to this inquiry: To whom do thoughts arise? Until truth dawns there can be no rest, until the ego atrophies in the pursuit of understanding. In either case, the fire for awakening has to burn so intensely that the separate self is abandoned.

Self vs. No Self

There is sometimes confusion between the Buddhist idea that there is No-self and the Hindu idea that there is only Self. Let's attempt an explanation.

The Buddhist idea that there is No-self means that there are no discreet entities, including the entity, "Solomon" (substitute your own name). Solomon and everyone and everything else is actually an interplay of infinite forces, a process not a thing. For example, (this is a take on the Buddhist doctrine of Dependent Origination, also elucidated by Deepak Chopra) I had peaches from the tree in our yard for breakfast this morning. This body is now literally constituted of those peaches which are being digested and their nutrients dispersed throughout the body. The peaches are juicy because of the rain we have had lately, rain which was absorbed by the tree roots and distributed to the fruit. The rain was composed of water vapor that evaporated from the surface of the ocean, say, somewhere off the coast of England. So this body is literally now made of water that a short time ago appeared on the surface of the North Atlantic.

Not to mention the minerals that were deposited in the soil by the movement of glaciers during the last ice age. The minerals were also in the fruit by the tree extracting the minerals from the soil. The minerals from the ice age glaciers are now fast being pumped by the heart to bathe cells in this body, so this body is somewhat constituted of the residue of earthly movements that took place millions of years ago. The glaciers were caused by ancient weather patterns cooling the earth. If we were so inclined we could trace the peaches in this body back to the big bang. If you want to bake an apple pie from scratch, it is said, you would have to create the universe.

Similarly, this book contains ideas that were spoken by the Buddha twenty five hundred years ago in India. The ideas spoken by the Buddha fill my thoughts, are here being further dispersed and, like seeds in the wind, like water vapor from the Atlantic, are spread by currents, intellectual currents. So Solomon on both physical and intellectual levels is a name given to an *infinite interpenetration*: not a discreet entity, but a momentary bubbling up from an infinite process. This fluidity, the fact that Solomon is more like a wave than a rock, is what is meant by No-self: no discreet Solomon, really.

As an infinite interpenetration, where does Solomon begin and end? Does he have boundaries? No, he is a bubbling up of an infinite process and so cannot be said to start here and end there. Solomon is a wave emerging from the ocean. As such, "Solomon," is a convenient concept, a name used to circumscribe an aspect of the infinite process, the name given to one momentary wave, but the name and the wave have relative but no ultimate validity.

However, all the currents of which Solomon is composed are fundamentally One Thing, the universe, the ocean bubbling up into a particular form. So while Solomon is a process not a thing, the I, the source from which Solomon derives his identity is a Thing (the One Thing, the ocean of Being) not a process; more like a rock than a wave, absolutely solid.

Solomon, the peaches, the ideas articulated by the Buddha, are all expressions of the fundamental reality, call it the Self. Each is a momentary bubbling up from the infinite process, an infinite interpenetration that is neatly circumscribed by a concept. But the infinite interpenetration that is named Solomon or Peach Tree, England,

Glacier, or Buddha is at bottom the One Thing bubbling up into a momentary form. That One Thing is the Self, and that Self is the imminent heart and fundamental nature of Solomon, Peach Trees and everything.

What is that Self? Call it what you will. God, Nirvana, Original Consciousness. The One Thing, the fundamental reality takes a zillion forms none of which is discreet, none of which stands alone, none of which is a thing unto itself; each is the One Thing bubbling up into infinitely interpenetrated appearances.

How did the Infinite get here in the first place? Why is there anything at all? I have no idea; that is the ultimate mystery.

Samadhi

Why is there anything at all?

Jim Holt, in his delightful book, "Why Does the World Exist?" asks the question, "Why is there something rather than nothing?" Why is there anything at all and not an eternal absence? While this may not entirely answer the question, I can suggest that the question arises only to the mind. When Consciousness in immersed into itself, when the mind is concentrated - let's use the Sanskrit term "Samadhi" to designate this state - the question does not arise just as the question would never arise in deep sleep. It requires separation, a movement of mind out of absorption for me to look at myself and ask, "Why do I exist?"

The philosopher Sartre talked about pre-reflective and reflective consciousness. When you are playing tennis and a 100 mph serve is coming your way, you better be pre-reflective. While entirely immersed in experience, waiting for the serve, you are not questioning your existence. If you stepped out of immersion to question your existence, or to worry about the bills, the serve would hit you in the face, or worse. From the perspective of immersion, meditative absorption, Samadhi, the pre-reflective state, the question "Why do I exist" simply does not arise; there is only Existence.

I suggest that Original Consciousness does not wonder about its own existence because it is a state of integration and unification. It requires a stepping out of Original Consciousness to question. But once this happens, there is a reversion to the very condition Original Consciousness transcends.

Perhaps the question, "Why do I exist, Why is there something rather than nothing?" is meant to inspire a search, the lover searching for the Beloved, and *the answer to the question is found in the state where the question ceases to arise.*

Subjective and Objective Truth

Western philosophy tries to reason its way toward truth, and a kind of truth about the objective universe is certainly available by reason. $E=MC^2$ is a truth of this sort. The subject looks into the object and observes its properties. This enables a manipulation of the properties of the objective world so that the benefits of science can be reaped.

But the East aims for a different kind of truth, a truth by which the subject is transformed, a truth that one *becomes rather than perceives.*

Nirvana is an Eastern paradigm of truth. One does not see Nirvana as an insight about an objective universe, one becomes Nirvana subjectively. That is why sages of the East say that when the Self is realized, many fundamental questions are answered. One becomes the state that is itself the answer.

In this sense, the Eastern conception is superior because knowing something does not necessarily solve my existential problem and so is only a partial truth. But an experienced truth provides both philosophical insight and existential relief in *moksha*, liberation.

Original Consciousness

You or your consciousness is the same as He and His Light, by which all else shines forth. (Talks with Ramana Maharshi. P. 317).

I once heard a guru, Mooji, make the statement: You were present at the big bang. That statement struck me as odd. What I can say on reflection is that, in meditation, with eyes closed and attention introverted, the sense of being the unboundaried Consciousness within which phenomena appear can become common, and carried over to the waking state. The sense of size and place is transformed. Previously, your sense of size is the size of the body relative to the external world, tiny. But Consciousness has no size and no reference point. Without a reference, without identification with the body, how big am I? *What is the size of Consciousness?* Without identification with the body, with the body as another phenomenon appearing within Consciousness - it could be said that all phenomena are the body, as all phenomena arrive via the body and its senses; is your true body, then, the world? - I am no longer small, rather I am that within which all things appear, *without which things would not appear.* Without identification with the phenomena that float incidentally in awareness, but rather as that within which phenomena appear the consideration arises: You are - this is - Original Consciousness.

Remember it is not the ego, the person, that is Original Consciousness. Ramana has said that "Consciousness purged of the mind is felt as God." The ego is not Consciousness, but a phenomenon appearing within Consciousness. Not the ego, but Consciousness purged of the ego. The ego is an accumulation of knots in the mind and body, energy blockages that restrict and inhibit Original Consciousness. To the extent the ego is undone, Original Consciousness becomes apparent.

The Feeling Compass

Depth of contemplation is equal to concentration of mind.
The more concentrated, the steadier the mind,
the greater the alignment in the chiropractics of the soul.
Why? Because dispersion of mind is the hallmark of misalignment,
like a signal with a lot of static,
whereas concentration of mind is a signal steady and clear.
Concentration is what Being seeks:
at-one-ment, a state of integration, the end of dispersion.
So concentration of mind is depth of contemplation, yes,
but is *felt* experientially as inner alignment and so bliss.
The less dispersed the mind,
the greater the inner alignment,
the more peaceful you feel as well.
Feeling guides the way toward truth.
Finding inner truth is the same thing as finding inner peace.

Metaphysical Musing

I have been reading, discussing and considering various world views, including the view that Consciousness is a by-product of matter; the brain creates the mind. Also the question, "Why is there something rather than nothing?" Both of these questions are fundamental and related. Though it may seem invalid, I use the feeling-compass as one way to determine metaphysical truth. By this I mean that I ask myself which proposition *feels* true? Does it feel true to me that I will dissolve into nothingness at death? That is the case if matter is fundamental nature. The brain creates the mind and, with the death of the brain, so too does the mind and Consciousness die. The materialist position is the atheist position: Consciousness depends on matter, on the brain, and the death of the brain is the death of Consciousness. While this is possible, it fails the feeling test. It does not feel true. Now, my feeling might only be a matter of bias or conditioning, like being a knee jerk Democrat or Republican; still I have no choice but to use this test. Why? Because I have never known myself not to exist. To suggest that life is a presence between the absence of birth and the absence of death seems false. I may not remember existing before a certain point in this life, but not remembering existence does not necessarily mean non-existence. I have no experience with and cannot remember a time that I did not exist, and so it feels to me as if I have always existed. I do not assume that I was born.

This is consistent with the suggestion that I am of the eternal. Eternity is my nature. I participate in That Which Is Eternal. I am of God, shall we say, and so are you, and so is everything. To me this feels right and truer than the proposition that I was born and will die.

Further this seem a better explanation for "Why is there something rather than nothing," than the existence of a purely material universe that exists for no apparent reason. Somehow it seems more likely that there is something-rather-than-nothing because Consciousness is eternal and is the fundamental reality. The alternative is that a material universe sprung out of nothing for no apparent reason, the material universe happened to generate life, and life happened to generate this little quirk of Consciousness. Though it does not really answer the question, "Why is there something rather than nothing?" (because we can still ask, "How did Consciousness get here in the first place?)" it seems a better answer that Consciousness is eternal rather than matter sprung out of nothing for no apparent reason (fortuitous accident Number 1), and the little quirk of Consciousness happened to appear (fortuitous accident Number 2) in a material universe.

In fact, I am not sure that matter exists at all. All I have ever known is Consciousness. Knowing *is* Consciousness. All anyone has ever known is Consciousness. To suggest that matter exists independent of or without Consciousness seems implausible. A universe without Consciousness is a lights-out universe, total darkness, a universe that has never been known or perceived; effectively non-existent. It seems more plausible to build an understanding of the universe on a foundation of Consciousness rather than on matter. If that is the case then everything is Consciousness, the fundamental reality.

Again, the contemporary argument of neuroscience is that the brain creates Consciousness, that *I am my brain.* This is the materialist argument. Consciousness is a fortuitous accident in a material universe. Without this fortuitous accident, there could conceivably be a material universe that has never been known or perceived. But is such a universe - a material universe without Consciousness, a lights-out universe of eternal darkness - really conceivable? Where does a material universe without any Consciousness exist?

The alternative hypothesis is that Consciousness is the primary reality. The scientist who studies the brain does so by means of Consciousness. The scientist who decides that materiality is the primary reality does so by means of Consciousness. The scientist's conclusion - that Consciousness is a byproduct of matter - is obtained by means of Consciousness. Atheism is possible only by means of Consciousness. This is *the God hypothesis*: Consciousness - God - is the primary, eternal reality which allows for the consideration of materiality, atheism and all else. Now, we still don't know how Consciousness, how God came to exist in the first place, why there is something rather than nothing, other than the answer already proposed: in Samadhi, in meditative absorption, the question disappears and we are left with infinite Being, the God state. Then God has returned to Himself. God recognizes Himself. The Lover has found the Beloved. From this perspective, the *where* question is also answered: the universe - *everything* - time and space - exist in the unboundaried Consciousness that I fundamentally am.

But let's get back to the feeling-compass. Truth is revealed in happiness or, at least, the truths that are most important to human existence. So it becomes important to feel your way towards truth; this is where meditation comes in. Western philosophy is an attempt to reason your way toward truth, but these truths, then, are purely intellectual. In the East truth is to be experienced; it is an existential, transformative truth. We can know truth through distilling experience to its essence: Being. So truth is found within by means of the feeling-compass. Peace, love, happiness, and illumination point the way.

If life and Consciousness are accidents in a material universe that arose inexplicably out of nothing, then my Consciousness is insignificant. I am basically like a bug in an enormous universe and when I die, well, many bugs die after all. While this may be true it does not pass the feeling test. However, if Consciousness is eternal and the universe is a staging for Consciousness, then my Consciousness partakes of universal Consciousness, then I am not just a bug but an actor in the cosmic drama, and it is through me and everyone that the universe gets to experience itself.

In a material universe, I am a very small and insignificant accident, a bug. In a conscious universe I am the opposite of a bug, I am large and significant for it is this Consciousness that brings the universe into Being.

The Heart of Religion

Lately the idea has been circulating that the world's religions are disparate and do not point to the same God. The religions are not different paths up the same mountain, they are each a different mountain. I am no fan of religion, which is as likely a detour as a highway to truth. Still, for religious scholarship to promote this view reflects religion's essential problem: many of its practitioners and scholars fail to see to the heart of their own subject.

Say a person has multiple personalities, all very different. One personality is aggressive, another is timid. One personality drinks, another is sober. One personality is sexual, another is prim. But all the personalities belong to the same person. Trace any personality to its source, trace any branch to the trunk, and you come to the same center.

The world's religions may seem very different, each with its own personality, but each religion is a bubbling up of the same infinite universe into a different form. This is the case not just for religions but for everything in creation. Every person, every animal, every culture, every continent is different, but all these appearances are bubblings up from the same underlying reality, the source and heart of all transient forms, the source and heart of the reader. That source can be called God and from that God there is never any separation.

This metaphor can be extended to another idea in circulation, the idea of a multi-verse. The multi-verse suggests that our universe, beginning with the big bang, is just one little universe in a much larger cosmos that includes many such universes, created by many big bangs. Why should there be just one big bang - ours - after all? There may, in fact, be infinite big bangs in an infinite universe. But all the little universes in a multi-verse, all the small U universes in a large U, all inclusive Universe, are like different personalities in a multiple personality; but all have the same source. All the small U universes are branches that extend from the same trunk; there is a common source and unifying principle. And this unifying principle is the essence of all its productions. So the principle that unifies, the source and heart at the center of a multi-verse remains the source and heart of all its transient forms, including each small U universe; and is the source and heart of the reader. That source can be called God and from that God there is never any separation. That source is the essential identity of the one reading these words.

The Tree of Life

Earlier we used the metaphor of a tree to indicate the structure of the mind. The mind's many thoughts are like the many branches in the canopy of the tree, but all the thoughts emanate from a single source, the trunk, the "I." Let's stay with the metaphor of the tree but with a twist.

Let's say that the universe as a whole is like a giant oak, the great tree of life. And the forms of bodies, you and I, we are each expressions of that universe, like leaves on the tree.

This means, first, that you and I are not separate. We are equally leaves on the tree. Not only are we not separate, we are offshoots of the same Being. The tree expresses itself as one leaf or another. Thus, when looking at another person, that person at heart is literally the same Being as myself, and compassion is always in order.

At a more superficial level, it may seem as if we are entirely separate beings, separate leaves, without connection. At a deeper level it may seem as if we are brother and sister leaves. But at heart we are expressions of the same universe. The universe bubbles up to look at itself through many sets of eyes.

I once heard Papaji reconceptualize the notion of arrogance. Arrogance is usually the case when I make much of myself. It would seem to be arrogant to say that, at heart, I am the Original Consciousness. I can imagine someone saying, "how grandiose!" But Papaji's interpretation of arrogance goes like this. It is arrogant for the leaf to think that it is *not* the tree. It is arrogant for the leaf to think: "I am a separate entity, separate from the tree. I have an independent existence. Humph!" For, in fact, I am entirely dependent on the tree, there is no "I" separate from the tree, it is the "I" of the tree expressing itself as the "I" of the leaf. There is only the tree, the universe. So arrogance is actually asserting my independence as a separate entity. In reality, there is only the supreme reality and I am an expression of that supreme reality. Everyone is one way the supreme reality expresses itself, nothing less. Every leaf, every person - in fact everything - is nothing less and nothing other than the supreme reality expressing itself.

The Heart is the All. When I find my own heart I realize that my heart is the All. For this reason, in India, the mantra "aham brahmasmi" - I am Brahman, the supreme reality - has been recited for millennia. This is, I believe, what the Bible intends when it says: you are created in the image of God. You *are* the image, the expression of God, nothing less.

There is just one misunderstanding to anticipate. It is not that the ego is the supreme reality. Yes, the mind and ego are also expressions of the supreme reality, as is everything. That being the case there need be no bother about the mind. The universe is doing its thing, and one thing it does is give rise to thoughts. The mind will disappear when it is not given juice, when I forsake the arrogance of being an ego, which is also to forsake suffering. The mind and ego remain the primary obstruction, a misperception, like a mirage. So it is not the ego, the leaf, that is the supreme reality, the supreme reality becomes experienced reality as I relinquish the arrogance of being an ego, as I relinquish mind and settle into heart, the deeper nature of pure Being prior to any conceptions, and there discover that the "I," divested of ego, divested of the illusion of separate individuality, has its source in the All. The life of the leaf is not other than the life of the tree, the totality.

The Vegetable Garden

I haven't gardened for years. But the girls are older now, two in high school and driving, and two away at college. Not only is parenting less necessary, parenting has been uninvited! So I dug up the old vegetable beds and am excited about growing some of my own food. Fruit trees planted years ago yield bumper crops of peaches, and I planted apricots, figs and persimmons this spring hopefully to bear fruit in the future.

It is amazing that by simply placing a seed in the soil life begins to grow. I am particularly impressed with the bush beans. I did nothing more than place the seeds in the soil an inch or two deep. There is plenty of rain in Massachusetts so, in a few days, little crook heads pushed their way through the soil, straightened, and stretched toward the sun.

They grow on their own. The little seeds have become plants that will produce fruit, seeds, and the cycle will continue.

What turns the seed into a plant? By what power does the plant push through the earth, effortlessly to fulfill its charted course, as I do nothing but watch?

Papaji says, in the terms of our last metaphor, that it is arrogance for the leaf to assume it is separate from the tree. *The tree lives the leaf.* It is arrogance to assume you are an independent Being, that you are not lived by, an expression of the infinite universe. By what power does the heart beat? By what power do the lungs breathe? By what power does the brain think and orchestrate the organism? Though it may seem at first like arrogance to say, "I am lived by the One Life," on reflection it is arrogance to say I am anything but that. The One Life is living through this form as through all its forms.

CHAPTER VII:

NO DISTANCE TO CROSS

This chapter is composed of musings that straddle two perspec-
tives on the cosmic journey. From one perspective, we progress
as souls over time, growing ever more mature spiritually as we ascend
toward the infinite, our ultimate source and destination. From this
perspective, there is a progression through birth, death, and rebirth,
and a growing closer toward truth, toward God, during this ascent
through higher planes and realms of existence. However, from another
perspective, the non-dualistic perspective, there is no time, no birth,
no death, no movement, and no growing closer to anything. Can you
grow closer to Now? Has there ever been any distance from Now?
Can you grow closer to yourself? Has there ever been any distance
from yourself? From this perspective there is no distance to cross.
Distance is the very misperception to be overcome, as it perpetuates
the belief that something not already present needs to be attained. In
fact, what is required is the very stopping of the effort to attain, as this
effort unnecessarily roils inherently still waters. There is no distance

at all. Be still. You are and have always been what you seek; you have always been home; God has never been absent or distant, for God is identical with your Being, the I Am within, which becomes increasingly apparent precisely as movement ceases.

If there is a progression, it is in dispersing the clouds of confusion that obscure the ever present, imminent sun of Self. If there is a progression, it is to progress *in the stopping*, so that the roiled waters of mind return to stillness. And yet, returning to the first perspective, this stilling the turning of time is a profound, perhaps infinite progression for, as stillness deepens, the infinite shines ever more radiantly into the individual and social life. Can there be finality to the emergence of love, happiness, and wisdom in an infinite universe?

The Three Realms

According to Indian philosophy there are three worlds, three vibratory realms in the Creation: the physical, astral, and causal realms. Corresponding to these three realms, we are encased in physical, astral, and causal bodies. Like Russian Dolls, the physical body is smallest, encased in the larger astral body, which in turn is encased in the largest causal body. *

According to this philosophy, at present, while we are in the physical realm on earth, we are encased in all three bodies. At death we shed the physical body and so lose Consciousness of the physical realm. We are then encased in the astral body (with the causal body latent) and become aware of the astral realm, a vast heaven compared to earth.

However, if a physical pull remains, after a period of time spent in the astral heaven, we are reincarnated in a physical body and return to the physical world to learn what the physical world still has to teach.

The cycle continues. While I have a physical body I am aware of the physical world. At death I drop the physical body, lose awareness of the physical world, and become aware of the astral, a magnificent heaven free from the scourges of physical existence, unencumbered by the burdens of physical reality, a place following an entirely different and freer set of laws.

However, if any attraction to the physical world remains, eventually I reincarnate back in a physical body. When I evolve to the point that the physical world holds no interest, I am done forever with physical reincarnation. I have graduated from the physical.

Water seeks its own level and the soul ascends to vibratory realms that are compatible with its vibration. As the soul's sensibilities are refined, it ascends to higher worlds. Even on earth, there are many subcultures that I can associate with depending on my preferences. When getting drunk on weekends seems like lots of fun, I hang out with my drinking buddies in a noisy club. When inner truth seems more appealing, I may stay in a silent meditation center far from the worldly noise.

There are similarly many astral worlds in the astral realm at different levels of refinement, that the soul can visit depending on its level of development. As the soul becomes increasingly refined, it inclines toward higher and more refined astral worlds.

At astral death, for the soul already graduated from the physical world, the soul sheds its astral body and ascends to the causal world, encased in just its causal body. The causal world is even more magnificent than the astral, exceedingly refined, subtle, celestial, barely separated from the Infinite Source. However, if any pull toward the astral remains, the soul again dons an astral body and "reastralizes," just as previously the soul reincarnated by re-donning a physical body.

When no astral interest remains, the soul sheds the astral body at astral death, and graduates forever from the astral realm, coming to reside in the causal realm, separated from the Infinite Source by the thinnest of veils. Eventually the causal body is permanently shed and the soul merges forever in and as the Infinite Source.

The astral world has a different set of rules. Desire is difficult to manifest in the physical world where matter as unwieldy as molasses must be moved. Publishing this book, for example, began with an idea but many obstacles had to be overcome and matter moved before the book could actually appear in your hand. In the astral world, however, desires manifest immediately. If I want to be in a particular place, I am instantly there simply by desiring. This is comparable to dreaming, as we will see. In a dream I can be in Hawaii instantly simply by conjuring up the thought of Hawaii.

In the higher, causal world experience is seen to be thought itself. Experience is seen to be not real but idea. The idea of a universe appearing, say, in the very mind of God *is* that universe. So all this that I take as real is like a dream, a thought in mind at the highest levels of Consciousness.

While on earth we are encased in all three bodies, and so participate in the characteristics of all three bodies. The physical body is the animal body. We are focused in the physical body while employing the physical senses and enjoying sensually. The astral body is the more interior capacity of imagination and desire. The causal body is active in the even more interior and refined capacities of abstract thought, creativity, and contemplation.

We are centered in each of the three bodies in the alternating states of waking, dream, and deep sleep. While waking, we are centered in the familiar physical body. During dream, we are no longer aware of or centered in the physical body; rather we are centered in the astral body and are subject to the rules of astral existence. If, in my dream, I want to return to Hawaii, I am instantly there simply by conjuring up the thought. I am able to fulfill my desire simply with imagination.

In deep sleep I am centered in the causal body, closer in, closer to the Source. In deep sleep I am entirely without boundaries, limitation, and suffering. The conventional mind is absent, refined to pure Being. My batteries are recharged as I connect to my very source.

Now, why do I say all this? Because, using this framework, *the three bodies and realms correspond to the three stages of spiritual practice.* Negative-thinking corresponds to the physical realm, Positive-thinking to the astral, and No-thinking to the causal.

Negative-thinking corresponds to the gross, physical plane and the mundane, unconscious mind that runs by conditioning alone. It is the lowest level of mind and existence. In Positive-thinking, the mind is used more consciously. Positive-thinking is the elevation of mind to its astral capacities. I am able to liberally use desire and imagination in Positive-thinking, as I am able to do so in the dream state and, supposedly, in the astral heaven after physical death. And just as there are levels within the astral world, there are increasingly refined uses of Positive-thinking. At subtler levels I can simply hold an image in mind - whether a visual or verbal image, like a mantra - and resonate to that finer and subtler vibration.

The even subtler No-thinking practices are causal. No-thinking abandons the use of the gross mind and imagination for pure Being, just as deep sleep abandons the astral world of dream. As Ramana said in the quote that opens the chapter on No-thinking, thought takes you farther from the Self because the Self is more intimate than thought. Thoughts emanate from the Self. Similarly deep sleep is more intimate than dream; the causal more intimate than the astral. The highest causal contemplation of No-thinking is mind distilled to its essence as pure Idea, pure Intelligence.

*For a detailed discussion of the Three Realms and the process of the soul's migration among them, on its journey back to its Source, see Autobiography of Yogi by Paramahansa Yogananda, chapter 43, The Resurrection of Sri Yukteswar. Meher Baba, in his magnum opus, God Speaks, also offers a very detailed description of the soul's ascendance among the three realms. Eben Alexander, MD, in the near death experience described in his book, Proof of Heaven, seems to corroborate the characteristics of the astral and causal realms, though he terms these realms the Gateway and the Core, respectively.

The Spiritual Fair

Rebecca is a seeker. She went this week to the holistic health fair and encountered its many displays: crystals, Reiki, psychics, shamans, meditation, and other healing practices. While all are lumped together under the term *"spiritual,"* I tried to make a distinction among kinds or levels of spirituality. Using the model just described, I would probably categorize crystals and psychics as astral, while Buddhist and non-dual meditations are higher, causal practices. Just to delineate, to refine the categories among all the booths presenting at the spiritual fair.

Happiness Review

In deep sleep you are, as they say, happy for no reason. In deep sleep there is an inherent happiness and not because anything has been gained. In fact, you have nothing at all. Deep sleep is the peace of water without any wind. It is the peace of Being itself, the peace of wholeness, silence, quietude, inherently radiant, requiring nothing, depending on nothing. This happiness is not dependent on desire, it is precisely the absence of desire. Desire would be a ripple on the pond in the pure, causal happiness of Being.

But if the pond does ripple and the mind awakens into dream, there is the potential for the fulfillment of desire. In dream there is, potentially, the happiness of an imagined heaven, of life just the way

I would like, Hawaii, all my dreams come true, a perfect movie: the perfect house, the perfect companion, the perfect car, the perfect setting, the perfect life. This is the happiness of perfect conditions, all my desires fulfilled: astral happiness.

In the mundane waking state, there is trouble because I may immediately return to negativity and obsessing about my dilemma. When I stir from the perfect peace of deep sleep - the unconditional happiness that depends on nothing but comes from my nature - or the conditional happiness of dream and the heaven of perfect circumstances, in the conventional mind I return to a state of obsessing, problem, and suffering.

So my job in the waking state is to avoid Negative-thinking, the mundane mind, and to anchor mind in higher contemplation, say, to see archetypal beauty in everyone I meet, to see perfection in all circumstances, God in all things, to see through a lens of heaven, or to be still and remain the bliss of Being felt in deep sleep, to see this world as literally floating in air, literally floating in a sea of space, not solid and heavy but more like a phantasm, a vagary, a whim, floating in empty, endless Consciousness.

Intelligence

This book is a series of thoughts. Each sentence is another thought. How many sentences are there in this book? If I wanted to be obsessive, I could hit the Tools function in my word processor but - let's just say - lots. Lots of individual thoughts are comprised in this book.

Yet, from a higher perspective, this book is a single thought, a single idea. Once you have read the book and know what it's about, you can hold the idea of the book in mind without requiring that each sentence be revisited.

The individual sentences are the articulation, the spelling out of the idea of the book. But the idea of the book can be held in mind, and the idea contains all the sentences spelled out in the articulation that takes place over time.

Holding the idea of the book in mind is using the conceptual or, in the framework just described, the causal mind. At the level of the causal mind all the details, all the spelling out is contained in the idea of the book. All the sentences spelled out over time are *simultaneously contained* in the idea of the book.

Now consider an Infinite Mind. An Infinite Mind would simultaneously contain Everything. All the spelling out of every universe would be simultaneously contained in the idea of Everything held in - shall we say - the Mind of God. All the story lines of every universe and every person, animal, bird, fish, plant, worm, and microbe in every universe would be individual sentences in the (rather big) book, one thought after another that issue from, that together constitute the idea of Everything held in the Mind of God.

Yet I propose that *the Mind of God is your mind.* There is no difference. The Mind of God is not other than your mind. There is no you apart from the Mind of God. You are one articulation, one sentence in the book, one story line among a zillion others issuing from the

Mind of God, but your source *is* the idea of Everything dreamed up by the Mind of God. The mind of God is dreaming the cosmic dream, including the dream of you. As you ascend toward your own source you approach the Mind of God.

As contemplation ascends from Positive-thinking to No-thinking, from astral to causal, and as contemplation ascends within the causal sphere, mind becomes more and more refined, concentrated, lofty, elevated, simultaneously containing more and more within its purview, potentially ascending to its source in the Mind of God. To do so, I believe, is what the Buddha meant by Nirvana.

Or as Ramana has said, "Consciousness purged of the mind is felt as God."

In contemplation the mind is purged of dispersion. The roiled water is purged of its churning until only still water remains: pure Consciousness. The mind single-mindedly searches for and ascends to its source, which has always been its source, which it has never been other than. The dispersed mind is transformed from mere thinking to Knowing, from thinking to Idea, from thinking to sublime Intelligence.

From this perspective, it is not an ego who is writing because the ego is the mind's mundane conversation with itself. To the extent that mind is purified and transformed into Intelligence, it is not an ego writing but Intelligence communicating with Itself, in the form of the reader, by means of the writing.

Knowing

All my life I have known,
that there was something that I knew,
but I have not known what exactly it was that I knew.
Now I realize what I have known.
I have known my faculty of knowing,
my own *pure intelligence*, that is,
intelligence as essential to, as *identical* with my Being,
prior to any content, to any thing known.
I have not been able to put my finger on the specifics of my knowing,
because the function of knowing -
intelligence itself - is itself nonspecific.
Intelligence does not need to know anything in particular,
to know its own presence.
Rather, intelligence is Consciousness, it is *the capacity to know*,
and some of its wonder comes,
when intelligence recognizes and comes to rest in itself,
rather than in the world it illuminates.

No Distance to Cross

She conceived of the spiritual journey as a journey into archetypes.
"Spiritual" meant everything occult - the Tarot and astrology, for
example - with their images of kings and queens, gods and goddesses.

The archetypes are the big ideas. In the Kabbalah, the system of
Jewish mysticism, the universe unfolds as follows. The Unmanifest
Source decides to descend into manifestation. Beginning in the
Unmanifest as Limitless Light, the Source dons one veil of form, then
another. The Light is thinly veiled in the subtlest realms closest to the
Source. The Light becomes more densely veiled as it descends farther

into form until, in the physical realm, the veiling in form is most dense, and the Light is most obscured.

The archetypes are the pure ideas - Plato spoke of these, the Platonic ideas - the early thoughts in the mind of God. The very first thoughts in the mind of God, the first emergence of the One's differentiation into two, are perhaps the thoughts of Truth and Beauty, the male and female principles, the primary split of the One. Like cellular division in a zygote, the One splits into two, and the two further divides into the ten thousand things - using the language of the Tao. In other words, the One eventually descends into a fully manifested universe, just as the one celled zygote "descends" through layer upon layer of division until becoming a fully formed infant.

In the Kabbalah, the differentiation of the Limitless Light is complete in Malchut, Kingdom, the physical realm, the farthest descent into manifestation. On earth, the One has completed its descent in the fully formed bodies of the seven billion humans on the planet - as well as the other life forms - each of whom continues to have its source in the One.

This is an interesting idea. Because while, from one perspective, we can talk about levels of differentiation, and descent over time, from another perspective there is no time and nothing other than the One which has never moved. For example, while a movie may display many dancing images of light, describing an epic story taking place over vast historical epochs, all the images are only projections of the Light, and the Light has never moved. All the images are saturated with that Light, are plays of that Light, are variations of the Light that has never moved. From the perspective of the Light, there has never been any movement.

The appearances change but they are merely projections of the Light. So, while from one perspective we may be "far away" from the Source, "way down here" on the physical plane, seemingly the farthest planet from the Sun, from another perspective there is no, nor has there ever been any distance from the Light. We are, each of us, saturated by that light. There is *no distance to cross* and no return, just as there is no distance between the images on the screen and the light that animates them. The images *are* light. We have always been, and at this moment are, at one with, projections of, animated by the Source.

Since we are in this very moment projections of the Source, if we look for our own source we find *the* Source, we find that we are that very One. The Heart is the All. Similarly, we can find within us all the layers that the Source has projected in its journey toward the physical, including the archetypal.

Another metaphor for this mechanism is a prism. The white light source is diffracted through the prism into different wavelengths, purest in color closest to the source, more diffuse as the diffracted light becomes more distant from the source. Close to the source we find the purest idea of blue or red, and these colors become less pure the farther from the source they travel.

Her spirituality is about the big ideas, the archetypes. But, I suggest, why not ascend beyond the archetypes to the source itself?

Why stop at the archetypes? Ascend to the pure Light: to whom do the archetypes appear?

The Infinite Spectrum of Diffracted Light

Julia is a college student with a brilliant intellect that she applies within her field of interest, the Philosophy of Art. I suspect, as a career, she will teach and write about art in academia. In a presentation for one of her college classes, she said, she talked about Mondrian and his painting.

As she spoke about Mondrian, I pictured his abstract painting in mind. Something about the abstract nature of the art triggered a series of insights. I saw that art is a reaching back to and representation of the archetypal. Mondrian painted the archetypal that he saw. Mondrian painted the archetypal the he *was*.

I imagined that the Creation is a diffraction of the Infinite Light. We are each wavelengths within the Infinite Spectrum of Diffracted Light that is the Creation. The created universe is the Infinite Light diffracted into the Infinite *Spectrum* of Diffracted Light. Each one of us is a unique band, a unique color within the Infinite Spectrum, having our source in the Infinite Light.

It could be said that the Infinite Light diffracts into many vibratory realms, many worlds. Within each realm – say, within the physical realm in which we live - are many beings each of whom is a further diffraction of the Light, a unique bandwidth in the spectrum. Every being is a unique diffraction, a unique bandwidth of the Infinite Light, having its source in the Infinite Light.

Mondrian is one bandwidth in the spectrum after the Light has been diffracted into creation. In his art, he is representing the unique "color" in the Infinite Spectrum that he sees and is.

Great sages (the Buddha or Ramana Maharshi, for example) are like the sky with no clouds. They are transparent to the Divine. The personal self has been entirely dissolved so the Infinite Light shines through without obscuration. Great art similarly has little obscuration. Great art is a pristine representation of the Light. The greater the art, the higher it reaches, the more the Infinite Light shines through without obscuration, the mightier, the more beautiful, the more breathtaking.

Julia too is one vibratory expression of the Universal Light. She too, in her lifetime, will project her beauty in the world, an intellectual beauty. She will find her place within the collective and give her gift.

But life goes two ways. Not only with Julia contribute her light, not only will she give to the world what she has to offer, but she will take from the world what the world has to offer. She will live and learn and grow and in doing so will refine, she will ascend and grow toward the Universal Light or, rather, her obscuration will dissolve and she will better know her own source in and as the Infinite Light.

Bardo

My wife and I had dinner with dear friends whom we see too infrequently. After dinner, we sat for dessert in an outdoor café in Harvard Square, as the café was near closing. Not having seen them for some time, I asked my friends, "What do you think about," a question I often like to ask. Susan said she thinks about death. Her mother died early, at age fifty, and the number lurks in her thoughts. Time may be short; besides the Catholic teachings of purgatory from her childhood, and the more recently encountered Tibetan teachings of the bardos, both inspired apprehension. If death was not navigated gracefully, the soul might wander in intermediate, sketchy planes of existence. "What do you think?" Susan asked.

Well, those are the only teachings that seem to suggest there is any reason for fear in the after death experience. Everything else - especially the literature of the near death experience, where the body dies for a while before being revived - suggests that, if anything, beauty is to be expected. No one ever wants to return to this world from the near death experience!

I believe the fundamental nature of the universe is love - Susan agreed - and that love is most densely veiled in this earthly realm. If that is the case then, upon departing this realm, love should only be more apparent, more radiant, the veil that much thinner. A realm with more apparent and vibrant love might await, a heaven, and probably heavens beyond, higher and higher heavens, where infinite love is scarcely veiled at all.

My wife said she believes there is complete cessation after death, like the cessation of anesthesia, a very deep sleep. That is certainly the case if materialism is true, if matter is the primary reality and Consciousness is only a byproduct of matter and biology; an accident, really, of chemical processes in the brain. If Consciousness depends on matter, when the brain dies, Consciousness dies.

But it seems apparent, even as I sit here in Harvard Square eating a brownie, that I experience only Consciousness. Everything is saturated by the light of Consciousness and I experience only modifications of that light. The world and all seeming materiality is a play of light. After death, the light will animate a different movie, even as it does now from moment to moment, but I believe that light is primary, inviolable, and will continue to shine, but mediated by a body with characteristics suited to the plane it will inhabit.

The End of the Race

I have participated in many races - not very well, mind you, a weekend warrior - running races, group bike rides, triathlons. The races can be grueling. There is a point in the race when exhaustion and doubt set in, the onset of survival mode, just hanging on, drained, running on momentum. The race seems interminable - and why do I put myself through this anyway? But often, just past the exhaustion phase, the realization dawns that, in fact, the end is approaching. Interminable though the race may have seemed, by now most of the ground has been covered. The miles have ticked away; the home stretch is approaching. The end is no longer abstract but is graspable, finite. I can locate myself in relation to the end, just past the next mile or over the next hill. My spirits lift. I shift up a gear and give what is left of my kick.

Approaching sixty, I start to feel this way about life. Like the race, life has seemed a process that would go on forever. I have known about the end - death - but the end has been merely theoretical. I have been immersed in the drama of the race, the drama of my life, as if it would never end, taking its plots and subplots very seriously. Until now: I can actually locate myself in relation to the end. I sense the finish as an actual event.

And the effect of this realization? At times: the greatest joy. Like the race, life has sometimes been arduous. The realization that the effort will soon be over is wonderfully joyful. An end to the consternation and brutality of this life, its tribal mentality and warfare: from this perspective, how comical their seeming significance.

Because: what will be beyond this life? Into what will I dissolve? And this too brings joy. I believe that I will emerge in something magnificent. Earthly life is like a boat on the ocean. I have lived within the confines of this little boat, from railing to railing, but soon my boundaries will expand. My world will be not the world of the little boat, but the immense ocean on which the little boat floats. I recall where I may have come from and to where I may go: something much greater and radiant.

But consider: is not this world an expression of that radiance? Is that greatness absent now? Can this world be other or apart from that greatness? Then I am outside the perspective of time, of death in the future, of a progression from here to there, and there is only eternity, it is ever present, it is present now, it is what all this is. Then I see God alone, and see God everywhere, but *I* do not see, for there is only God and no other, only life in all its exquisite beauty, from every blade of grass to every distant star, and this world with all its apparent failings is magnificent, is divinity itself.

A T-Shirt Slogan

I am nearly sixty years old. I (this body) will be dead in 30 years or so. Not that far off. Just a matter of a little time.

Everyone on the planet, more or less, all seven billion will be dead in a hundred years. Not that far off either. Pretty rapid turnover. From this perspective, life's dramas are not to be taken too seriously. They will all end shortly one way or the other.

Michael suggested we come up with a T-shirt: *Don't fuss. We'll all be dead soon anyway!*

I like it. We'll make a fortune.

The Deathbed Cry

I read that on his deathbed, he cried out in doubt.
Those who heard the cry felt pain for a life ended in uncertainty.
But if there is light on the other side of death,
that cry was soon to be followed by splendor.
And so the deathbed drama is poignant,
only from this side of the crossing.
Having crossed, the poignancy that provoked the cry,
must certainly have turned to laughter.

Eternity

Deirdre's spirituality has a Christian bent. She brought a popular evangelical book to our session and read passages from the book to me. The book seemed to say that eternal life will begin after death, in heaven, for those who made the proper choice on earth - accepting Jesus as their savior, I suppose. Those who did not make that choice during their earthly sojourn will not participate in eternal life. We did not read too far into the book but I can only guess what awful fate might await those who do not agree with the author. I'm in big trouble!

It all sounded so very odd. How can eternal life begin after death in heaven? Isn't eternity by definition that which always is, which never is not? Eternity must exist *now* and always. It has never not existed; it can never not exist. How can eternity begin at some time in the future? What begins at some time in the future *cannot* be eternal life, because whatever has a beginning is in the realm of change and so is not eternal; whatever has a beginning must also have an end. Eternity is always.

I presented one of Ramana's metaphors to Deirdre. Ramana says that life is like a movie that is always changing, but the screen on which the movie appears never moves or changes.* It is permanent. The screen is not affected by what goes on in the movie, but the movie could not appear without the screen. The movie appears in the context of the screen. The screen is the unchanging support that makes the changing movie possible. The screen is the eternal source from which the movie of life springs.

The screen can be thought of as the Now, which never moves, or as the I, which always is. Has it ever not been Now? Have you ever known yourself not to Be? The I-Now is the unchanging context within which life appears.

In fact, *I-ness and Now-ness are the same thing - that "thing" is the eternal and - surprise - like a game of tag - You are It*! You are Infinity, Eternity looking at itself through a particular set of eyes.

After earthly death, the movie of life will probably continue, and continue to change. It will probably become a heaven realm, a spectacular movie, Avatar 3D. But a heaven realm is not eternity; it's just a much better movie. Heaven will still appear *in the Now, to the I* - in the context, against the backdrop and, we could say, "made" of Eternity. The Now and the I are unchanging; the true meaning of Eternal Life, *present even now*, present always.

Deirdre said this discussion reminded her of an elevator she once rode. The elevator was made of clear glass and was situated on the outside of the building, affording a wonderful view as it rose. The view, she said, became more and more wonderful, but the person in the elevator - the I - was the same all along.

Brilliant! Let's explore this metaphor. Say the elevator begins in the garage and rises to street level where only the facades of the neighboring buildings can be seen. The view is very mundane in the garage, and is only slightly better above ground.

But the building is very tall. Eventually you rise above the neighboring rooftops to see a panorama of the city. Then you see beyond the city, the surrounding suburbs and landscape, all the way to the horizon.

Let's say this building is infinitely tall. You rise higher and higher into the stratosphere, then into space. You practically brush the orbiting moon, a comet whizzes by, you are deep in the solar system, there goes Jupiter!

You rise beyond the solar system into the Milky Way, sprayed by stars and nebulae. Beyond even the Milky Way, behold the galactic dance of the spiraling billions. Heavens lay spread before your gaze but, as the celestial spectacle unfolds, the seer in the elevator has never moved.

The mundane movie may change in highest heaven into a spectacular movie, but all change appears within the unchanging Now, within the unchanging I, the context for change, *which exists now and always*, Eternity, your own Heart.

*Earlier the unchanging was compared to the light in the projector, while here it is compared to the screen. The light is the unchanging from the perspective of the Heart; the screen from the perspective of the All; different ways of saying the same thing.

The Unchanging Screen

Ramana Maharshi's metaphor - the world is like a movie that appears on the unchanging screen of Consciousness - allows something and nothing to exist simultaneously. The something is form, the movie of life in all its rich complexity. The nothing is formless, the unchanging screen of now, of I Am, of Consciousness, that does not and never moves. So the perfection and simplicity of nothing is as present as the messiness of something. And ultimately, he would say, you are both of these, the unmanifest and manifest, the formless and form, at once.

Reprise: Peace

A breath is born and dies;
it rises and falls within my Being, but I Am not moved.
A day is born and dies;
it rises and falls within my Being, but I Am not moved.
A lifetime is born and dies;
it rises and falls within my Being, but I Am not moved.
A universe is born and dies;
it rises and falls within my Being, but I Am not moved.
I Am at Peace.

Science and Spirit

On streaming media, I have been watching the Cosmos series with Carl Sagan. Cosmos is a series of thirteen hour-long programs, first aired on Public Television in 1980, in which Sagan wonderfully brings scientific inquiry to a popular audience.

I cannot but admire the scientific impulse he embodies and describes so well: the impulse to wonder, the desire to know the truth. Essentially Sagan asks and tries to answer the questions: What has been the progression of the universe from its beginning, from the initial burst of creation (if in fact there was a beginning)? How and of what elements did the galaxies and stars form? How did the planets form and come to orbit the stars? How did life begin on our earth and what has been the progression of life on earth from single celled organisms to man? And has a similar progression taken place on any other planet elsewhere in the universe?

Spiritual inquiry arises from the same impulse: the desire to know the truth. But the domain of spiritual inquiry is not so much the outer, observable universe as the inner world of the observer. Who am I? Who is the observer, the seer, and what is the relationship between the seer and the seen? It is interesting that Sagan, whose wondering ranged so widely, nowhere seems to ask: who is it that is wondering? What is *his* nature?

From this point of view, there is no difference between the impulse toward science and toward spirituality. They are equally endeavors aimed at discerning the truth. And there can be no conflict in their conclusions: what is true is true. Science and spirituality are sister attempts to discern the ultimate nature of things, but looking in somewhat different domains with somewhat different methods.

In fact, all fields of knowledge are attempts to know the truth, but the slice of the pie that each field looks at is different. Still, all the pieces of the pie - natural science, social science, spiritual science - must fit together. It is the same universe that each inquiry considers, though each may look at a different section of that same universe. And just as the insights in the fields of natural science - biology and chemistry, for example - dovetail, all truth from every domain must fit together just as nicely.

I think the premise of the spiritual perspective is that everything is fundamentally Consciousness. Everything, it seems, is made not of atoms and the components of atoms, but of the Consciousness that perceives the atoms and all else. Atoms appear within Consciousness so Consciousness is primary. Everything is "made" of Consciousness. As you read these words you are experiencing nothing but Consciousness and the contents that happen to fill your Consciousness at this moment: atoms, air, tables, chairs, sensations, thoughts. Anything that anyone has or will ever experience is Consciousness.

In a dream everything is "made" of mind. There is no substance to the dream, however it may appear. If you are straining, lifting heavy rocks in a dream, still, the heavy, seemingly solid rocks are made only of dream-stuff. So everything that now appears substantial is similarly "made" of Consciousness.

If there were no Consciousness to perceive it, would a universe exist at all? Is a universe without Consciousness conceivable? A universe without Consciousness would be of no benefit, no value, as there would be no one to know, to experience, or to wonder at the universe. Can a universe without Consciousness, a universe that has never been perceived, a lights-out universe even be said to exist?

Which brings us to a second premise of the spiritual perspective: the universe is here for some benefit, for the benefit of Consciousness. In other words, there is significance in the universe existing, it serves the purposes of Consciousness. If there were no Consciousness to experience the universe, it would benefit no one and nothing, and truly would have no significance, a literal non-event.

So the two premises, the two hypotheses, the two faiths of the spiritual perspective are that 1) all is Consciousness (what seems to be materiality appears within Consciousness and so is actually "made" of Consciousness) and 2) the universe exists for the benefit and purposes of Consciousness and so has value; it is not a meaningless and indifferent event.

Don't be put off by the F word: faith. Science too is founded on belief. Any scientific hypothesis is a matter of belief. An experiment is then constructed to see if the objective world confirms the belief; to see if the world works the way I think it might. If the experiment is successful then what had been belief is no longer mere belief, it is true, it is confirmed as fact. My intuition has been borne out by reality.

The spiritual intuition is exactly the same: I believe something might be true, something others claim they have confirmed in their own spiritual research, and I go about the business of confirming whether this belief is true in my own experience.

Just as science attempts to verify its hypotheses through experimentation, the method by which spiritual research is conducted is meditation, introspection. Consciousness starts to notice itself. Attention pays attention to itself. And while outer exploration is enhanced through the use of instruments - telescopes and microscopes to see the large and the small more clearly - Consciousness sees itself more clearly through concentration, attention focusing intently. And what is the effect of attention focusing intently? Distraction is eliminated, the busyness of mind is eschewed, and so the busy mind subsides through intentional focus, mindfulness. What is left? Consciousness is distilled to its essence: pure Consciousness, Nirvana. And Nirvana is perhaps the ultimate nature of things, and their significance.

In the East, the nature of reality has traditionally been described as Sat-Chit-Ananda: Existence-Consciousness-Bliss. Bliss or happiness has perennially been described as being the nature of reality, the nature of Consciousness. This is very important - the very essence of the spiritual perspective. For if there were no happiness in the nature of things, if happiness were not the ultimate destination of Consciousness, then the universe is as much nightmare as blessing, as much hell as heaven. A universe that is fraught with suffering has no significance; such a universe we could do without. Then we might conclude that Consciousness is an accident in an accidental universe. An accidental universe is indifferent and, in such a universe, suffering is as likely as joy. Who needs it?

But a universe where happiness is inevitable - only resolve the chiropractics of the soul, just get yourself lined up right - a universe with a happy ending - we can say that such a universe has significance: it exists for the benefit of Consciousness, for its eventual happiness. Then we can say suffering served some purpose - like the obstacles in any romantic comedy that lovers overcome before they are eventually united in bliss.

Remember that the Buddha begins the Four Noble Truths by affirming the reality of suffering. But he goes on to say that suffering is only a stage in a process that ends in Nirvana. The destination of Consciousness is Nirvana, ultimate happiness. That is the testament of the Buddha and the faith required to undertake the rigors of the spiritual journey.

If the mechanics of the objective world are the proving ground for scientific hypotheses, what confirms the truth of spiritual hypotheses? I would suggest that illumination and happiness are the hallmarks of success in the spiritual inquiry. The spiritual journey begins with the sense that something is not quite right. Some truth remains unseen and some happiness unfelt. I am compelled to proceed by the sense that something is presque vu, almost but not quite seen. But if I proceed successfully, I will come upon illumination and joy. Truth will be revealed in happiness. Happiness, then, is the compass that points toward and indicates the presence of truth. Follow its star.

Spiritual truth is confirmed by happiness. When the chiropractics of the soul are not in place, I suffer. Intuitively I feel that something is out of joint. When the chiropractics of the soul are in place, I say, "Ah, this heart of joy is how I was meant to feel."

The faith that propels the spiritual journey forward is the intuition that there is meaning, there is significance in the universe existing, in *my* existing, there is something beyond suffering and, by pursuing the cosmic inquiry, that significance will be found, and its taste will be joy. This has been proposed by the masters and, like directions given by a reliable authority, I choose to follow those directions, trusting that I will arrive at the same destination. I will know that destination by joy, for such is the taste of truth, and the worth of the journey, the significance and meaning of existence revealed. This is the spiritual hypothesis. May it be universally realized.

CHAPTER VIII

THE FRAGRANCE OF GOD

Dear reader: We hope you have enjoyed the tour. We have arrived back at the terminal: the journey's final Destination is the same as its Source. It has been a great pleasure sharing this time with you. Please disembark the bus once again. In the terminal, near the exit, is a gift shop of fragments. Take some time to browse, if you like. You will find, in different sections, various souvenirs of the tour which are available for your purchase. You might like to bring a memento home with you. Have a safe trip and thank you for taking our tour.

A. Fragments

Vastness

In the encounter with vastness - that which stands on earth for, that which stirs within us the remembrance of things eternal - in meeting the thundering ocean or pristine desert sky, with all their timeless beauty and equally timeless indifference to the machinations we are so passionately involved in, there is also then an encounter with our limitations, preoccupations, self-possessions, our worries over past and future; there is an encounter with the fact that there may be painfully little room in mind to accommodate the vastness. For the immensity is in the present, and available only with a renunciation of all that qualifies our present. But the recognition of the need for a renunciation is already the sign of a collaboration, a resonance, a communion between the vastness seemingly without and the vastness within.

Karma

While the fellow who plants a flower one afternoon clearly enjoys the many pleasures immediately involved in the planting, it can be said that he is responsible for the pleasure of all those others who witness the flower he has planted long after he is gone; that a certain measure of delight has come into being as a result of his original action. Accordingly, we would do well to consider our actions carefully, especially if the cosmic mechanism is such that we reap the fruit of our actions; even until the effects of which we are ignorant.

Progress

When I think back on the course this life has taken I realize that, though I have knocked on many doors, only a few doors have opened to allow for the forward progress of aspiration. I am where I am because of the rare confluence of desire and opportunity.

Common Sense

Swami Satchitananda used to say, while teaching yoga, "Before learning to stand on your head, learn to stand on your feet."
Reb Schlomo Carlebach used to say, "You need to have a good heart. You also need to have a good nose."

The Rains

The rains came after Sunday softball. We took shelter high in the vacant stadium, beneath the overhanging cement roof, where we both were sheltered from and could witness the great storm and the spectacle of nearby lightning and thunder.

When I was a child God seemed very great, very powerful, and distant. Coming to know God seemed certainly to involve traversing a vast terrain, undergoing much hardship and austerity. The exalted Moses got only to see the shadows of God's passing, for no man could look upon the face of God and live. God was like that, enormous and beyond.

Recently I have come to entertain the possibility that God might be near, very near, nearer than my own breath, an intimate, myself in fact, the core of my Being, not difficult but simple to know. Only be still and sense the Being that is always already there. It only made sense that God should not be the result of some ordeal. I would lie in my hammock under a canopy of trees, leaves would flutter and dance and whisper in the wind, clouds would float across a diamond sky, the hammock would rock, oh, so gently, moved I know not if by wind or if by the pulsing of my own heart. God was like that: a gentle voice, a gentle laugh, a chickadee, a hummingbird.

But high in that stadium the skies spoke with power, and if the truth is a butterfly it also shakes with thunder the earth and structures of man, very near and very far, closer than a heartbeat, and the most profound of all things to comprehend.

Rorschach

We had too many players for softball that day, and one player from the fielding team needed to sit out each inning. I sat with the hitting team when my turn came. There was a close play at second, the batter tried to stretch a single into a double, and the tag was put on at second. All of the batting team leapt to their feet and shouted, "Safe!" All of the fielding team shouted, "Out!" I among them, a solitary voice on the bench, for my sympathies belonged with the team on the field. Everyone looked at the play through their bias, their predilection.

The candidates are running for president; the debates are on. The Republicans see the Democrat and, in their hearts, they are shouting "Out!" The Democrats see the Democrat and, in their hearts, they are shouting "Safe!" The Democrats look at the Republican candidate and see a nit-wit. The Republicans look at the same man and see virtue. We look at the world through a bias. By interpretation we create what we see.

Heaven

The religious view that says, "Heaven comes after life on earth," seems to me superficial. Because if there is heaven only after earth, after death, then a corner of experience remains that is unredeemed, where the potential for suffering remains. That is, return to earth (or what earth represents), and suffering will again be there. A stain of ignorance remains within the individual psyche that would revert to suffering under the right conditions. The truth is more like, "Until you can turn earth into heaven you are not yet a profound soul." Spiritual development suggests that heaven is maintained even in the domain of hell, even in materiality. Heaven so pervades your Being, there is nowhere in the universe, no realm, nor circumstance that can deprive you of that bliss.

Like Ramana Maharshi: the insects that ate his legs while, as a youth, he meditated in the temple vault; the cancer that ate his aged body; neither made any impact on his absorption in God.

Space

Richard Branson is planning to shuttle people into space, and I understand the desire for that sort of incredible experience. But when

Consciousness is refined, still and powerful, you could be sitting in your backyard, or at work, and be ecstatic. There is no need to seek exotic experiences however beautiful they may be, because when beauty is within, beauty is seen wherever you look.

Everest

The statement of craving is: *"It should not be happening this way."*

The statement of realization is: *"Nowhere is there a greater beauty."*

In other words, there is no need to climb Everest, to search for some ultimate experience elsewhere, for one is already and perpetually at the summit, and yet the beauty of the view is ever different, ever new; for every new moment is a new summit.

Hamlet

Hamlet had it right. The basic question is: Do I want to exist or do I want not-to exist. Asking whether one might want not-to exist implies that existence - or earthly existence, the existence we know - is burdensome and one might prefer to be without it.

I have said to depressed patients and I might say to Hamlet: It is not the body that needs to die, the body is not the problem. It is *the mind* that needs to die, for mind is the repository of suffering. It is possible for the body to remain intact and yet for the mind to renounce suffering, to drop every thought, every burden, every sling and arrow. If the mind does swear off preoccupation, the possibility of happiness while in the body arises.

The death of the mind is perhaps the best of both worlds: one gets to exist and not-to exist simultaneously.

Facebook

At times I notice in myself the desire to reconnect with intimates of old: old friends, old flames. I think this is a desire to relive the magic that once arose between us, when our two souls recognized each other in beauty, recognized a commonality and connection and, like one flame lighting another, the world was transformed into love. I suppose, if the desire is very strong, that may be inner guidance that there truly is something more to be lived in the relationship. But more often than not - in this age of the internet when any old friend can be found - the original magic was unique to the moment when our two lives spontaneously met, and all machinations we may try now to relive that beauty will only result in awkwardness.

Still, there is a new moment now, redolent with magic, as destiny unfolds afresh. There is no need to revisit the past. We are intimate with this present moment which bears the fragrance of reality; magic is eternally available and at hand as the very nature of Being.

What is Wrong with this Moment?

There is a temptation to think that happiness will be found by *doing* something: calling a friend, going to the movies, going to the ocean or a vacation home, and that may be true. But if I feel discontent and that something must be done to assuage the discontent, I must question the impulse and ask, *"Why is this moment insufficient?"* Will not a moment in a different set of circumstances be insufficient for much the same reason?

I Am

Like a drone in music, a tone that persists unchanged below the flights of melody, the drone in human experience is the tone *I Am*. Before recognizing this tone what attracts attention is the melody of life, the excitements and disappointments, the themes in major and minor keys. As one settles in - to life, to oneself - the volume on the underlying drone of *I Am* increases. It moves from an undertone, faintly heard, barely acknowledged, overshadowed by the lines of melody, to a more dominant and powerful tone that saturates the melodies above. And this is a good thing for *I Am* is a beautiful sound, a sound of peace despite change, and refuge despite insecurity. So long as one is, it can never fail and can never be distant.

Hubbub

I want to know God. I want to know something of truth, peace, purity, and beauty in a complicated world, a world of travail. I want to know whether something pristine, unsullied, can be found in the midst of this hubbub of life.

How to know God? The how is in the wanting. Want to know; that is all. In the wanting, in simply posing the question with desire and passion, attention is directed in some new way, in a way that knows that it does not know, that asks "how" without preconception, and in the suspension of the known, in suspending the hubbub itself, there is room for the unknown to make its presence felt.

Stars

There are New Age teachers who teach only fulfillment. Their lives are successful and they teach the principles of success. No mention of adversity is made, as if adversity signaled unenlightenment. But is it not more realistic to suggest how adversity is to be handled, especially given the state of this world?

Through history, writers have complained about the times they live in, as if the age they inhabit were uniquely benighted. It seems that *this* age is uniquely benighted. I was walking in conservation land and passed a man fishing. "I am a tree hugger," he said, "I come here to get away, I can't stand to listen to the nightly news, it makes me depressed." I commiserated that media avoidance is necessary for mental health. Depression follows from the events of the day for many.

So, in times when many are cognizant of struggle and war, it seems rose-colored to speak only of the lavish abundance available with proper application of the principles of abundance; the reign of heaven may not come to pass in our lifetime.

I was camping at Cape Cod recently and would, each night, go to the ocean to look at the stars before retiring to my tent at the campground. The skies were clear and the stars were breathtaking. I remembered why the Milky Way is called that, the rim of the galaxy thick with stars and their white luminescence. Though we live in the country, I see that milkiness only on the Cape, by the ocean, separated by the width of the Bay from the lights of the population centers. Looking at this embarrassment of riches in the sky, it is easy to imagine that the source of the nightly splendor should appear equally on earth to fill the lives of women and men. The New Age teachers of abundance say it is only our misunderstanding of universal principles that prevents the splendor of the heavens from filling the earth.

Still, whether times are prosperous or not, or in times of adversity and war, it is enough perhaps simply to remember the stars and what their splendor represents. The stars are concealed during the day; one would not know there were stars at all. When darkness falls the great secret is revealed, the cosmic context of awe, the enormous beauty that surrounds our lives but is obscured in the light of day.

Try to remember that context during the daytime when the drama of life is overwhelming. The backdrop to the stage of human life, and the heart of all things alive, is the great beauty that upholds.

B. Practice

Practice and its Fruit

Every practice yields its fruit. If I practice guitar daily, I will become a monster guitar player. If I practice my jump shot, I'll get nothing but net. If I exercise, my body becomes stronger.

Positive-thinking changes the image held in mind for the better. It is quite possible that affirmations, for example, produce their unique effect by changing your resonance, and situations vibrate in tune to your resonance, like iron filings that align themselves along the path of a magnet. It is possible that affirmations intended, say, to create prosperity may aid in creating prosperity. The practice geared toward prosperity yields its unique fruit.

But enlightenment comes from a different quarter. The practices of No-thinking yield the taste of eternity. The masters of eternity were not prosperous in a conventional sense, nor were they physically fit. That was not their concern. Their teachings have a different, higher emphasis, bearing a higher fruit.

I suppose both practices - Positive-thinking and No-thinking - and others can be undertaken, each yielding its fruit. There is no reason you cannot be enlightened, prosperous, and a monster guitar player who can hit his jump shot.

Medication of Meditation?

I often say there are two ways to improve mood and state of mind: medication and meditation. Medication will provide a relatively quick fix and is one tool in the toolbox that is certainly worth using. Beyond medication, beyond changing the brain's biochemistry, is meditation, using the term "meditation" in the broadest sense. Beyond the biological fix, all that remains is what can be done inwardly: mind acting on mind one way or another. Even if medication is used skillfully, once medication has done what it can, all that remains are the gains that can be made inwardly.

Don't get me wrong. Those gains are enormous. The inner world is vast and the mind powerful. I prefer that patients undertake the inner discipline when possible. But true inner change requires dedication: a profound desire to overcome limiting patterns of thought and bad mental habits. For some reason, people are happy to go to the gym and undertake physical discipline. Weight loss and the perfect body are very motivating. Mental health for some reason is less so. If the same energy that goes into the gym went into the mind, the drug companies would themselves become depressed, as fewer prescriptions would be written.

In the case of substance abuse, if the door is closed on the substance as an option, if I close the door on alcohol, for example, then I must deal with whatever I was avoiding by drinking. The energy that was funneled into drinking will have nowhere to go but forward, as I directly encounter my life issues. For some, if the option of medication were withdrawn, they would have to deal inwardly with whatever causes depression or anxiety.

I sometimes suggest that patients go on silent meditation retreat at a reputable retreat center, but this suggestion is rarely taken. On silent retreat - and I am simplifying - there is nothing to do other than to be present and to observe the mind's tendency to go off into past and future, the elsewhere. Because there is nothing else to do and no distraction, the mind's bad behavior becomes more evident and the ability to withdraw from preoccupation becomes stronger. Bad mental habits are weakened; healthy mental behavior is strengthened.

If I learn to play the piano, the new finger movements are as if hard wired into my neurology. My body has learnt something new. My fingers find the keys without effort. But the new knowledge is latent, evident only when I sit to the piano and play.

In meditation the neurology also learns something new. But these new skills are skills of awareness. Because I am always aware, these skills can always be exercised. They do not require a particular time and place, as does sitting at the piano. Because thinking always takes place in the greater context of awareness, I always have the opportunity to utilize the skills learnt in meditation. They are skills of life.

While many people go to the gym or take piano lessons, they are less likely to undertake mind training, possibly because it is less culturally understood. I suggest introducing meditation and mental health skills into the school curriculum, as much as music and physical education. I see my children spend so much time in busy work that will not ultimately benefit them much. Learning to discipline the mind in the ways of awareness will teach skills that actually contribute to a lifetime of well-being.

C. Art and Beauty

The Great Unifier

A great artist is able to convey a beauty so fundamental that the art is appreciated by people who diverge seemingly in every respect, other than their appreciation for the art.

The appeal of a great leader similarly cuts across diverse constituencies: blue and white collar worker, natives of the heartland and coast, forces for slow and swift change, all are united in their appreciation, all turn to the leader with hope and trust.

The appeal of archetypal art or the archetypal leader cuts across every constituency: so deep, so absolute, so persuasive, so undeniable is the message.

Such is the great unifier: that in which all recognize the divine reflection.

Escapes

Many artists have used their art to escape the confines of a limiting life. The culture the artist is born into might normally steer him toward working in the coal mines, unloading or building ships at the docks, or working in a prosaic family business. But success in art - or athletics, another form of art - allows an escape into a rarefied world unimagined by those who simply acquiesce to the culture of origin.

In this art offers two forms of escape: social escape through the doorway to new opportunity; and transcendent escape into the joy of the art itself, the act of creation; escape from the ordinary mind into mystery, accessed through the gifts mystery has itself bestowed; an escape independent of the social outcomes the art might produce.

Birth Pangs

Art, he maintained, is meant to challenge the prevailing ethos, to shatter structured and limiting ways of seeing the world. In performing this function it will necessarily be uncomfortable as the familiar is undone.

Of course, I agree. There is always discomfort in stretching one's capacities and doing so, like running a marathon, is ultimately exhilarating. The question is whether the art is dissonance for its own sake. When Stravinsky premiered the Rite of Spring the audience howled. The music was dissonant but, as the ear adapted to new tonalities, the work came to be appreciated as beautiful. When Einstein proposed Relativity, the Newtonian conception of the world was shattered, to be replaced by an even more sublime, truer, more far seeing conception. In both cases the sublime was challenging the conventional. A higher truth was calling and the discomfort felt was the birth pang of the new. But to violate for the sake of violation is not necessarily art. The sublime may not be calling to a higher revelation at all; the dissonance is uncomfortable because it expresses not beauty but its opposite.

Elegance

Write as you speak, she said.
No, I like to write with some elegance.
The world I see is elegant.
The patient drift of clouds across the sky is elegant.
The mosaic in the dappled clouds is elegant.

The half moon rising above the pine cover,
into blue sky is elegant.
The white of the moon alongside the white of the clouds is elegant.
The blue shading of the cratered moon is elegant.
The tapering of the pine trees upward is elegant.
The movement of leaves in the wind is elegant.
The sound of leaves stirred by the wind is elegant.
The seed pods falling from the branch are elegant.
The sunlight fragmented through the trees is elegant.
The corona of the diffracted sunlight is elegant.
The knock of woodpeckers on the dead oak is elegant.
The yellow finch flying with a seed is elegant.
The counterpoint of the chickadees and crickets is elegant.
The soulful chant and dive down of the mourning dove is elegant.
The sound of my children playing, all are elegant.
The joy I feel in being is elegant.
I see an elegant world and would like to write in its fashion.

Philosophers - even the best philosophers - see ideas and deal in
the currency of ideas; they see formulae, schema, conceptual glory. I
would rather contemplate the natural glory of the Eden with which I
am surrounded, forsaking mind and ideas altogether, lost in the sensual embrace of life.

Burning Tree

Moses saw a bush ablaze,
that wasn't eaten by the flame.
This autumn day I saw the same.
A maple lighted up in red,
which nearly glowed, and clearly said -
that tree of fire in my gaze -
the miracle once spoken of's,
still present to the eye of love.

Beauty

The case is being hotly debated in the metaphysical courtroom. Evidence on both sides is presented before the judge and jury. Is life a meaningful expression of divine intelligence; is life spiritual? Is life material - are we merely incidental offshoots of material processes that happened to produce life and Consciousness? The jury is split, the verdict could go either way. But the defense calls one more witness - "We call Beauty to the stand" - and in comes Beauty. The courtroom gasps; everyone feels the scales decidedly tilt. For if the universe were an accident, if life and Consciousness were merely incidental, then why is everything so beautiful? Beauty betrays intelligence, dare I say beauty is what love looks like. The sensual and intellectual beauty of the universe radiates from and expresses the character of its source. Trace beauty to its source and one finds pure beauty, pure love, pure intelligence. The verdict is in, the case decided, the contestants spill out of the courtroom to face the media.

Robert Hughes, the late art critic and avowed atheist, once said that he looks for art to astonish, to induce a state of astonishment, and I can well understand what he means.

We live in the woods. In the depths of night, in summer, I may step out of the French doors of my bedroom to walk beyond the backyard among the trees. I enjoy this nightly sojourn. I look into the night sky and am astonished. I hear the aural hum of the crickets and katydids, the earthbound Om, the music of the earthly sphere, and am astonished. One need look no farther than the natural world to be astonished, to be overwhelmed by Beauty, but I cannot then be both astonished and an atheist. Beauty has spoken; the matter is decided.

D. Social Affairs and Closing

Violence

The TV has been showing an ad for the new movie by a famous director. The ad contains a series of clips each showing the movie's star engaged in an act of violence. He is either punching people - a close-up of his clenched fist rapidly approaching - smashing things, or shooting guns in a rage. These clips are the film's highlights, meant to attract people to the theater.

How sick is that? The director, who is considered a great film-maker, is almost universally a purveyor of violence as is the actor, his compatriot. They seem to revel in the most graphic cruelty one human can inflict upon another and, for this "artistic" contribution, are showered with awards and adulation.

Ram Dass once wrote that dictators could not rise to power if people were not cut off from their deeper selves. The same is true of the culture in which we live, a culture that cannot recognize truth and its absence, a culture that adores men for squeezing every last grimace and drop of blood from an act of violence, a culture that takes this for great art, a culture lost.

Driving home from a recent holiday, an NPR interview with another director crackled through the radio's poor reception in the remote

White Mountains. The director was elaborating on the notes he had hand written into the screenplay for his latest film. The notes described how one must feel during the act of strangulation, how intimate it is for one being to strangle the life out of another. The discussion was given considerable air time, apparently meriting the serious reflections of the artist. I looked at my wife and we turned off the radio.

There is scarcely an American film without a gun or explosion, the hallmarks of American cinema. How childish! Recently we have been watching world cinema: Cinema Paradiso, Kolya, Live and Become, Lemon Tree, The Red Violin. These are beautiful stories of the human condition none of which feature gratuitous violence, simple stories simply told, requiring no pyrotechnics or strangulation, yet deeply moving. Sadly, the market in America for these films is small. Instead, our director will probably win an award for his latest contribution to our culture, where a clenched fist and oozing blood are taken for things of beauty.

Guns

In the heaven I go to after I die, I imagine love will reign. As the Dalai Lama has said, heaven will be a place where spirituality is apparent. Spirituality will be in the air you breathe, the light you see, the music you hear, the fragrance you inhale, the atmosphere of love, peace, kindness, and beauty. In some descriptions of the heavenly realms, hearts are so filled with joy that joy can hardly be contained. Such is the nature of heaven.

Now, imagine that a gun is introduced into this heaven. With the introduction of the gun, fear, violence, and death are introduced. There is not love and communion but separation and suspicion between the one pointing the gun and the one - man or animal - at whom the gun is pointed. Heaven has been tainted with the taste of hell. A heaven with guns is not my idea of heaven.

I suppose there are many astral realms and we can each go to a realm that suits us. In my heaven there is no inkling of a gun. In someone else's I suppose everyone is packing. But, again, that sounds to me more like hell than like heaven. Why would anyone need a gun in a realm of love?

Let's return to earth and the gun debate. What kind of earth do we want to create: the hell of everyone packing, or the heaven of love where even the intimation of a gun lowers the vibration, inserts a bit of hell into heaven?

On earth many levels of Consciousness coexist. There are both sinners and saints among us. We need to be realistic and, for now, a certain use of guns must be tolerated; a professional use of guns perhaps by the military and police. We must acknowledge that lower Consciousness may intend harm and be prepared for that possibility. But this requires only a limited accommodation to the reality of ignorance; society on the whole should continue to move in the direction of heaven. As Consciousness evolves* it will evolve not toward the hell of everyone packing, but toward the kingdom of heaven on earth where no one is packing, where even the hint of a gun, the introduction of fear and violence into the rarefied atmosphere of love is disdained.

Some advocate for guns on the basis of sport and I suppose that is legitimate: guns as an instrument of play. But it is nearly impossible to separate guns as instruments of play from guns as instruments of death so, for practical purposes, it is best to restrict play in the interest of restricting death. Play hardly seems worth the price.

So what kind of earth do we want to create, a heaven or a hell? I believe, as Consciousness evolves, in a hundred or a thousand years, guns will spontaneously disappear. No one will want or need a gun in a heaven on earth, where Consciousness has evolved to the point that its essential nature of love is fully manifest. Guns will spontaneously disappear when they are seen as distasteful. That may seem remote but consider that just one hundred fifty years ago half the population thought it perfectly acceptable to keep other humans as slaves; now no one thinks that. Someday no one will want a gun. For now, however, it seems wise for conscious governance to nudge society toward heaven; to legislate toward the elimination of hell and guns from the face of the earth.

*It is truer to say not that Consciousness evolves over time in humanity but, like clouds that disperse before the sun, humanity's confusion disperses which allows the Eternal Light to shine into human affairs with less and less obstruction.

Cosmic and Political Law

The universe is and works a certain way. Science is one attempt to discern the way that the universe works. As science discerns the laws of matter, it can apply its insights in the creation of satellites and TV's. But insight into the way things work also needs to be applied socially, so that social law mirrors cosmic law. Just as there are proper chiropractics for the individual, there are proper chiropractics for society, and nations needs to align with cosmic truth for happiness to flow in the social order.

All is One. What I do to another, I do to myself. It is accepted that it is generally immoral to kill. To a finer sensibility, killing and all violence is abhorrent, inconsistent with cosmic law, painful to witness let alone to execute.

As society evolves, the social law comes to mirror cosmic law more and more closely. At one time, slavery was thought to be acceptable. A generation ago, it was acceptable to hit your children. One day, as we evolve, we will stop mistreating, killing, and eating animals.

For all is One. What I do to another, I do to myself. Realizing this, policies will move increasingly toward the politics of universal compassion. It is inevitable, only a matter of time before truth prevails as society awakens. Because all is One, I believe it is also only a matter of time before the United States of America gives way to the United States of Planet Earth, a glorious transition, fit for fireworks, as the planetary order aligns with the cosmic reality of Oneness, as human Consciousness evolves to the point that it recognizes the obvious, if we should live that long. The universal awakening of love, of the heart may then signal the kingdom of heaven come to earth.

Vegetarian

It is difficult for me to take seriously the philosophical conjectures of someone who eats meat. Because if a person's sensitivity has not evolved to the point that he rejects the cruelty involved in killing creatures to satisfy his appetites, if killing creatures for pleasure does not offend, then that person's world view is fractional at best.

I was inspired recently to read about Scott Jurek, the ultra marathoner, who runs hundred-mile races (four consecutive marathons!) and is a vegan. Obviously we do not require meat for health; the body is capable of great strength on a vegan diet. So, if killing for meat and the whole industry of organized cruelty to animals, who are regarded not as sentient beings but as mere objects to be killed for carcass, for their meat, which is deleterious to our body's health in any case, is not instinctively offensive, then something primitive remains in a person's consideration of life.

The slaughterhouse: Auschwitz for animals.

The Devil's Masterpiece

Many fundamentalists hold primitive - even violent - views with great enthusiasm and set out to implement their views. Only when standing devastated in the rubble, holding their first born child dead in their arms, might they begin to consider whether their views were correct. The implementation of ignorance is undertaken with certainty because religion stands behind it. Religion is *the devil's masterpiece*, his greatest ruse. Thinking you act in accordance with the Most High, you set out to war, gleefully orchestrating the destruction of your enemy. Embarking on a course with a passion reserved for the Most High, you further the cause of the darkness.

But I suppose that is the purpose of this world, to see the word made flesh, the idea made actual, to see that the outcome of the seemingly religious ideal is the death of your beloved. A reconsideration is then in order, the ideal rethought, redrawn to more accurately reflect the real, whose nature surely is closer to forbearance and love. But how many more centuries of warfare must we endure before the religiously self-righteous awaken?

Post-Atheism

If you realize yourself as Spirit, you will see that this world is only spiritual and not physical. (Talks with Ramana Maharshi. P. 246).

"God is dead," Nietzsche said, and with that proclamation the stage was set for the eventual rise of a new atheism founded on science. Nietzsche foresaw the increasing irrelevance of conventional religion which was, as often as not, a force for tribal identification, separation, and conflict; the antithesis of the truly religious ideal of universality and love. It has since become fashionable, especially with the rise of neuroscience, to be a new atheist and assert the preeminence of science, materiality, and Consciousness depending on the brain.

Following in the footsteps of Nietzsche, I would like to proclaim the death of the new atheism, not to return to religion but, in the spirit of science, as an accurate assessment of the nature of the universe which is, I suggest, spiritual as a matter of fact.

Science is about the discernment of truth. There is sufficient evidence to call materialism into question, both in the literature of the near death experience, and in the perennial testimony of spiritual masters. As evidence mounts for Consciousness, spirit, and God as fundamental reality, even from within the discoveries of science, atheists will call the evidence into question. But this questioning is behind the curve, like the death throes of the dogmatic religion foretold in Nietzsche's proclamation, like the death throes of any counter-evolutionary agenda that clings to an ethos transcended by the forward impulse of Consciousness.

The Evolutionary Forward Impulse

The evolutionary forward impulse is the movement of Consciousness as it awakens within the individual and collective human body. Krishnamurti has said that intelligence is sensitivity and, as humanity evolves, it becomes more sensitive and intelligent. Coarse ideals are eschewed in favor of more sensitive, more compassionate ideals reflecting greater wisdom. But as Consciousness awakens it does so more dramatically in some individuals and societies than in others, and there is often tension between the awakened and those less awake. Waking rubs sleep the wrong way. Inertia is made uncomfortable by the glare of light streaming as into a darkened room, and resists. Only later, when unconsciousness stirs, does it abashedly realize what the light was illuminating all along.

There are many examples. Jesus and Socrates both ran afoul of entrenched social beliefs and only later, after being put to death, were they regarded as great seers.

Galileo was considered a heretic for proposing that the earth was not the center of the universe. The church placed him under house arrest until his death.

The church, no doubt, regarded itself as the embodiment of virtue and Galileo of heresy. Religion often thinks that it possesses the truth when, in fact, it may be the very embodiment of ignorance. (Even the great Pope Francis, whom I deeply admire for his solicitude toward the poor, regards the sexuality engaged in by our LGBT brothers and sisters as sin, a regrettably medieval and uncharitable perspective. Unless the church wants to posit celibacy as a universal spiritual ideal, and *all* non-procreative sex, including the sexuality of infertile and post-menopausal heterosexuals, as sin). Ignorance is ignorant of its ignorance. Ignorance does not know that it is ignorant. Why it believes it is virtue itself, in Galileo's time the mouthpiece of God on earth, a dangerous situation when ignorance also has power, as with Galileo and Jesus and Socrates. The power of the church and state were wielded against the bearers of truth and enlightenment with fatal results. This is the very definition of *evil*: the melding of ignorance with power.

Lincoln had to fight the Confederacy. Gandhi had to fight the oppressive British Empire. Martin Luther King had to fight Southern bigotry. Mandela had to fight Apartheid. Aung San Suu Kyi had to fight the Burmese military dictatorship, and so it goes with many movements in arts and ideas, or movements toward universal rights and social justice. Lincoln, Gandhi, and King were assassinated. Mandela and Suu Kyi were imprisoned for a good part of their lives.

Remember, like the Bruce Willis character in The Sixth Sense, ignorance is ignorant of its ignorance. Ignorance does not know that it is ignorant until it awakens.

In the examples above, awakened Consciousness rubs ignorance the wrong way and pays a bitter price for doing so, until the ignorance awakens and realizes its error, that it was always on the wrong side of history. I believe the evolutionary forward impulse generally manifests as a progressive political and world view, while unconsciousness manifests as social conservatism, the old and traditional which believes that it upholds virtue and is right to suppress the rabble rousers. But it is not. The Confederacy, the oppressive British Empire, Southern bigotry, Apartheid, and the Burmese dictatorship were never virtuous, on the contrary.

In social affairs, conservatism is often on the wrong side of history and does not know it is wrong. To say that social conservatism is wrong is to say that it is immoral; it deviates from the natural order of compassion and social justice. To combat historically conservative tendencies toward intolerance and lack of compassion, fierce battles had to be fought to abolish slavery, to establish women's rights, civil rights, gay rights, animal rights. Progressive Consciousness had to advocate for and overcome resistance from social conservatism until human

Consciousness as a whole evolved and moral truth became obvious. All the battles, say, for civil rights in the South now seem tragic and unnecessary. Looking back, why was a pitched battle required when it is now so obvious that our brothers and sisters of every skin color are entitled to the same love which we desire for ourselves?

Further, if "every thought you think you do to yourself," it should also be obvious that the kindest thing I can do for myself is to love others. When I do love, the climate of my psyche becomes loving. I have done myself - and everyone - a great favor. When I hate, when I discriminate, when I am selfish, when I am greedy, when I am unkind, I punish myself with my own unkindness. I will be happiest when I love, when I am generous, and so create happiness for others as well.

Today, for example, there are ongoing debates about gay marriage, climate change, health care, immigration. I suspect that, over time, as is often the case, the progressive position will become the established position. Soon resistance to gay marriage and the need to address climate change will be history. Eventually, I believe, like every other developed country, we will have government run, universal healthcare, the only moral system, as healthcare cannot be a corporate commodity designed to generate profit which, it turns out, is also a wildly inefficient system. The United States spends twice in GDP what other developed countries spend on healthcare. Yet the political climate in the United States cannot tolerate government in charge of *anything*, even when government presents both the moral and the fiscally sound option. Eventually, we will have a more tolerant immigration policy that acknowledges the suffering of the struggling poor, our brothers and sisters in the human family, regardless of the borders they were born behind. The immigration problem will be solved when all nations are free and prosperous, and there is no economic need to leave home, as prosperity is available everywhere. People will then move freely, north or south, east or west, as they do presently in the European Union, depending on preference alone. As public policy comes to reflect greater compassion and fairness, society moves more into alignment with cosmic truth, what Congressman John Lewis has called the Beloved Community, the community of kindness and of spirit.

Interconnection

During the last presidential campaign, Barack Obama made a statement that suggested business owners did not build their businesses solely on their own, and the statement brought about an outcry from the business community. Of course owners built their own businesses! But I agree with Obama and take exception to the outcry. Clearly there is great merit in the free enterprise system. But we live in an interconnected, infinitely interpenetrated universe. To ignore this metaphysical reality is to build an economic theory on falsehood.

Nothing arises on its own. Take any "object," your body for example. Your body is literally made out of the food that someone else grew on your behalf. You did not provide your own food. The earth grew the food. If we were to trace the arising of the earth that grew the food, we would have to go back to heavier elements ejected in the explosions of stars, themselves byproducts of the big bang. More locally, the food the earth produced was stewarded by a farmer, a human being with his own genealogy and personal story. The food was harvested using a tractor built in a factory. Each part of that tractor harvesting the food was built in another factory, and assembled into the tractor. The tires, say, were made using rubber that the earth had produced in a tropical rubber plantation. How did the plantation come to be planted? How did the sap come to be transported to the factory where it was formed into tires? How did the metal in the tractor come to be mined and forged into parts? Even to eat breakfast, an infinite number of factors and contributors come into play. This is the Buddhist doctrine of dependent origination. There are no objects, no discreet entities with discreet beginnings and endings; every object is a momentary crystallization of energy out of an infinite flow. It rises momentarily and will fall back into that flow. This is a metaphysical fact.

Think of the most mundane objects in your life and what needed to happen for those objects to appear. I just received a pair of jeans in the mail which I ordered from the Levi's website. The cotton had to be grown, (what historical convolutions must have gone into the ownership of the farm and planting of the cotton), turned into denim in one process, dyed in another, cut, labeled, shipped, and the internet and postal service had to be invented and their employees born and raised for those jeans to arrive at my doorstep. A seemingly innocent pair of jeans requires the collaboration of the entire universe.

So, in an interconnected universe, politics needs to be based on compassion toward all in the human kingdom, the animal kingdom, the natural kingdom, the earth, even kindness toward trees and plants. I will speak shortly about Amma, an Indian saint who is considered to be an incarnation of the Divine Mother. Her organization has been called an "empire." Yet hers is an empire of good, a model governments could emulate, an empire meant to eradicate suffering, an empire of compassion that has built orphanages, hospitals, and housing for the poor, that has taken sex workers off the streets, that provides health care, that advocates for animals, that stewards the earth, that has built universities with funding provided by the generosity of the more affluent who give freely, who see beyond their selfish interests and gain. Hers is a model for a spiritually enlightened society, a society of love. Someday that love will be expressed not only in pockets of spirituality, but will be fully expressed both in the individual, human psyche, and in the political structures the evolved human psyche creates.

Media

I lived as a Buddhist monk in Burma and Sri Lanka during the years 1979 - 1981. Burma was an isolationist country then, but I was fortunate to obtain a six month visa. At one point during my stay in Burma, feeling a desire to explore, I travelled by train from my base in Rangoon to Mandalay. I suspect that, in Mandalay, people had never before seen a white skinned monk. One morning I left the temple where I was staying to collect alms. The Burmese are very devout Buddhists; even so I was mortified that a Jeep had been enlisted to follow me as I walked, to hold all the abundant alms the surrounding throngs were offering.

I spent most of my time in Asia in silent meditation in various settings: meditation centers, remote village temples, or a jungle hermitage. In 1981, I was living in a meditation center when a kindly Sri Lankan gentleman, who served as an attendant to the monks, happened to mention that Ronald Reagan was president in America. That was news to me. I realized I had no idea who the American president was and, since I left the United States almost two years earlier, had forgotten that there was even an election.

What culture shock I experienced when I came home! I remember noticing on the bus ride from Kennedy Airport to Grand Central Station in New York, how insulated from the raw environment everything in America seemed. The roads were all well paved, the buildings all sturdily built, heated and air conditioned to protect against extremes in temperature, every suit well tailored, every foot well shod. In Asia much of the time bare feet tread bare soil, bodies were hardly clothed in the hot climate, homes made of mud provided minimal shelter, and roads were barely paved at all.

I gradually met back up with friends. Sitting with my old roommate from college, he lamented John Lennon's fate. "What happened to John Lennon?" I asked.

In the years before travelling to Asia, I had also spent several seasons in silent meditation. After a retreat in the Fall of 1978, I called my mother to check in once silence was lifted at the end of the retreat. My mother asked a funny question: "Are you involved in a cult?"

"A cult? What do you mean?"

"A cult!" she implored, "like the one in Jonestown!"

"Jonestown?" I asked, "What is Jonestown?"

At that time of life, I spent periods of months and years in reclusive meditation, entirely isolated from media. I found those to be periods of profound growth, grappling with issues of eternity.

There is no need to know about every bit of political wrangling that goes on day in, day out. Politics has become toxic. A patient I see who is addicted to CNN is among the most depressed, and for good reason. One could be oblivious not only to the minutia but even to larger political currents and be no worse off, as I was not affected when I was completely out of touch in Asia. On the contrary, while living alone on top of a mountain in the Sri Lankan rainforest, watching, from my rock, the waxing, crescent moon obediently following the sun down at sunset, its handmaiden stars sprayed across the sky, unashamed to shine alongside a moon so humble, beseeching the timeless to reveal Herself, so as to gaze upon the face of timeless beauty, I was quite happy to be entirely without the media noise, returning instead to the purity and bliss of innocence.

Technology

Many of today's innovative minds seek to better the world through technology. Social advance is seen to be almost synonymous with technological advance. Everyone is amazed at the pace of change and waiting for the next technological device and innovation. Yet if one wants to advance spiritually, I recommend going in precisely the opposite direction; for a while, put aside all technology which does little to evolve the fundamental human psyche.

In the attic I still have an Apple IIe, bought in the early 80's. I wrote my dissertation on that machine, and was happy to have it. I like my iPhone as much as the next guy, am writing on a laptop, and will distribute this writing through Amazon. Great stuff! But to develop spiritually, I recommend you put the smart phone away, disconnect from all media, and go into solitude in nature. Feel the rhythms of the sun's rising and setting, the rhythms of your organism, which technology may only obscure. Humanity's evolution is not just about the improved flow of information, but about connection with the cosmos. Technology may facilitate Arab springs, Occupy movements, and other outer change, but technology also facilitates a certain disconnection from the soul and, as such, is not an advance at all.

You want to know God? Put away the iPhone, turn off the TV and computer, stop networking, stop talking, go out of doors, be alone, for days, for months, let the organism settle into silence, listen to the pulsing of the summer night, listen to the pulsing, the longing and ecstasies of your heart, rhythms that are only drowned out by a relentless stream of superficial information. Technological advance does not necessarily evolve the human psyche. If humanity wants inner peace - which would be reflected outwardly as global peace - it should advance not only the speed with which information and goods are transported, but the transports of the human soul, and its intimacy with the imminent divine.

Amma and Krishna

I saw Amma,* the great Indian saint, at a public program last night. She travels the world to uplift humanity, literally embracing all who approach, spreading the succor and love of the divine mother.

In the course of her annual tour, Amma stops in Massachusetts each July. One year, she stayed in our home. Our family moved to a tent on the front lawn while she and her entourage took over the house. Port-a-potties peppered the property for the benefit of the thirty or so devotees she travelled with, all of whom slept on the floors of the house, packed in like sardines. Camping showers, large plastic containers filled with water that drain by gravity through spray nozzles, hung in trees throughout the yard so that everyone could shower. At the time, Massachusetts was the last stop on her North American tour. Before leaving for the airport at the end of her stay, a hundred or more devotees, all dressed in white, assembled in our back yard for a final program and send off. I wonder what the neighbors must have thought.

Last night during the program, the devotional chanting gathered force and fervor. The many blended voices rose in volume and urgency, as the synthesizer, harmonium, and tabla rose in tempo, all calling ecstatically to Krishna. Krishna is one of the divine incarnations worshipped in India.

Nyanamoli, a Buddhist monk and scholar, made the following observation. The rational West, where transportation runs on time, where highways are all neatly paved and divided, where markets trade in orderly fashion, and precise property lines are recorded at the registry of deeds, worships Jesus crucified on the cross, bloodied from his crown of thorns, blood pouring from his body, crying out to heaven in the midst of his Passion.

The East, where water buffalo share the roads with buses, and buses are packed with people like sardines, who hang from luggage racks and from out the doors, who nearly tip the buses from excess weight, where the poor live entire lives on sidewalks beneath awnings that provide their only shelter, worships the Buddha, a figure of implacable calm amidst the storm, of unshakable peace, unmoved and immune to the vicissitudes of life. For the East, where the material world is often in chaos, is more than passion enough, the divine archetype is Peace, finally.

Jesus and the Buddha are two archetypes of the divine. Another is Krishna, not so well known in the West but an archetype worth considering.

Krishna is often depicted playing his flute. Krishna is a god of play, of music and enjoyment. Krishna is charming, mischievous, whimsical, an enchanter. He is irresistible, a stealer of hearts, flirtatious, your perfect lover. Krishna is beautiful, with opalescent skin and, beyond his bodily beauty, he reveals the cosmic beauty, a timeless, kaleidoscopic display. Krishna is thrilling, the divine Beloved.

Krishna is an archetype very different from the somber God of the testaments, and even the sober wisdom of the Buddha, a soaring god of play and fun. The mind is freed from the shackles of convention in entertaining this divine form of joy, mischief, and play.

And then there is Amma. Amma is herself, I believe, a divine incarnation. She radiates unceasing love and happiness. I find myself continuously grinning in her presence, as one heart after another is relieved of sorrow in her divine embrace. She works tirelessly for the benefit of humanity; the wake of her love is enormous, spreading as from an ocean liner, touching so many with material or spiritual beneficence. I feel blessed that she stayed in our home.

Some await the millennial second coming and assume the divine will be apparent when it appears. But the divine and the forms it takes are creative. When the divine does appear it may not announce itself as expected, but requires discernment to see.

*After this book was first published, an expose was written by Gail Tredwell, Amma's personal attendant for twenty years. While Amma and her organization undeniably do much healing and charitable work, perhaps Amma is not entirely as she presents herself. A caution to be careful in spiritual matters.

The Scent of Joy

Melissa has several callings. To begin with she is a brilliant artist in oil and watercolor. She is quite literary. And she has been a compassionate lay pastor in her church. In that role she ministers to those in need, visiting and consoling.

When she was a child Melissa learned that, in order to be loved by her mother, she must be good. She must *do* good. If she was selfish, which was bad, love was withheld. Melissa was emotionally abandoned by her mother as a punishment for her seeming selfishness.

Melissa is so talented that she could be a significant painter. She would like to devote more time to her art and less to her role as a pastor. However, to do so is to do the thing that makes her happy and that is selfish, therefore bad. She feels obligated but not inspired to do good works. That is unselfish, therefore good.

Based on her early programming, following her heart's desire is associated with punishment. It is bad to let her spirit soar; that would be selfish. Doing her duty, albeit out of obligation, is associated with reward, with love. The thing that makes her happy yields abandonment. The thing that makes her unhappy yields love. It seems as if happiness is bad and unhappiness is good! Quite a dilemma.

In this case, as is often the case, the answer is not found in mind. Looking in the mind for the answer, like the man looking under the streetlight for his keys, is looking in the wrong place. The answer is found outside of mind for mind is precisely the problem.

Melissa, I want you to be like a bloodhound. You stand at a juncture. You can take one path or the other. Which path to take?

Follow the scent of joy. Stay hot on its trail. Let the mind be still and let the scent of joy guide you out of the thicket. Trust that joy indicates the presence of truth, a truth more authentic than the rote formulas of your programming. Ignore the clamoring of fear which screams: joy is bad, danger! That is hypnosis, not truth. Joy indicates the direction of *authentic* truth. In spite of what you were taught, consider that joy might actually signal goodness and, like a bloodhound, follow its scent, stay hot on its trail.

The Fragrance of God

Imagine you are walking along a street in town, or along a path through field or forest far from the ways of women and men, and you catch a scent in the air; there is a fragrance which is unexpected but strong, sweet, and delicious, (it could be lilac, honeysuckle or beach plum in bloom), and you wish to discover the scent, to find its source in the flower.

You follow in the direction of the fragrance as it becomes stronger, sweeter, more delicious still, searching through the interwoven greenery, sensing from the deepening scent yourself getting close.

Finally you find the flower, (many bees may be humming there), you lift up a sprig and inhale deeply; the scent is sweet, intoxicating; your head swoons slightly with delight.

The world is the Fragrance of God. The world wafts into space from its source in the divine.

Trusting the guidance that leads you, trace the fragrance of the world to its source; go in the direction where reality grows stronger, allowing yourself to become intoxicated as you go, as you inhale more of the deepening fragrance of reality, knowing that the fragrance always expresses the divine character of the source from which it emanates.

The Hearth

Imagine the seasons have turned; it is cold and you are outside walking down lanes lined with pine covered in snow, each dusted tree like a flower that waits for winter to bloom in this way.

Or you have been outside playing the winter games: sledding with children down the hill, skating on the frozen pond, skiing on mountains. Eventually you are chilled and the time to go indoors has come.

You enter the lodge and sense warmth emanating from somewhere in the great room; you sense a fire in the hearth somewhere. Instinctively, spontaneously, without thought, you move toward the warmth, toward the hearth, the lighted place aflame at the center of the dwelling. You find the hearth and stand there, letting the warmth penetrate to your bones, dispelling the cold.

Now, trusting the guidance that leads you, look inside your body for the place where warmth originates. *Find the hearth within the dwelling of your Being.* Instinctively, spontaneously, without thought, move in the direction of warmth, peace, comfort, fullness, and quietude. Find the quiet at your core and rest there, relinquishing everything superfluous and troublesome. Rest in your quiet, your peace, your beauty, recognizing this beauty as *your own Heart*; your very, inviolable nature.

Source

The source of the world saturates its substance.
The substance of the world reveals the nature of its source.
As fragrance reveals the nature of the flower,
and warmth the nature of the fire,
the unspeakable *beauty* of the natural world,
bespeaks the source from which it springs.
And what does beauty says of her source,
what does she say of the One who sent her?
Love; beauty says love.
Love, manifest, arises as beauty.

But beauty also says intelligence. Like any grand composition, the universe is a magnificent integration of form and content, engineering and aesthetics. There is intellectual beauty in mathematics, physics, science, the way things work; and aesthetic beauty in the appearance of trees and mountains, the moon and stars. The universe presents as whole cloth and all fields of knowledge - the disciplines that make up departments in universities - are individual threads separated out from the seamless tapestry, the perfectly-realized, cosmic masterwork.

Sacred Ground

But her body was invaded by cancer. Cancer filled her womb which
was removed to save her life. The sickness struck too close to her core
and she was frightened.

Where is sacred ground when the fortress has been breached?
Where is sacred ground when invaders take the hallowed ground?
Where is sacred ground when the bunker has been reached,
when the coffers have been plundered,
and the food stores have been found?

Though the surgery was successful, she was not at peace. She had been
invaded by cancer once, deeply, frighteningly, and began to doubt that
she would ever again feel safe.

Where is sacred ground when the body has been pierced?
Where is sacred ground when offspring have been razed?
Where is sacred ground when the temple is defiled,
and homes are set ablaze?

Where is sacred ground when the cemetery has been desecrated?
Where is sacred ground when the elders have been humiliated?

When the sky is filled with smoke,
and the sunlight turned to haze,
and the heavens have surrendered;
where is sacred ground?

Where can no one reach,
where can no sword pierce,
what can never fail,
what can no indignity defile,
what can never die?
There is sacred ground.

Belonging

In high school I hung out with the popular kids but I never really felt like I fit in or belonged, she said.

Isn't that the way it is? We move from one environment to another, from one social group to another, from one culture to another. And while we may fit in reasonably well, in some groups more than in others, even within our own families, isn't it true that the perfect fit, the perfect sense of belonging, the sense of being perfectly at home is only found within ourselves?

Relax. You belong to yourself. You fit perfectly, and have always fit perfectly, like a glove, within yourself. Enjoy the peace of being at home. And if you carry this sense of being at-home-within-yourself wherever you go, like a turtle its shell, you will find you fit perfectly always and with everything.

Reprise: Beauty

Let your own heart sing for you need no other song.
Yours is the beauty for which the sun rises.
Yours is the beauty the stars attend.
Yours is the beauty for which winter compromises,
the fields wave,
the waves rush,
and the rushes bend.
Yours is the beauty the worlds have come to celebrate.

REFERENCES

Alexander, Eben. Proof of Heaven: A Neurosurgeon's Journey into the Afterlife. Simon & Schuster, 2012.

Baba, Meher. The Everything and the Nothing. Sheriar, 1996.

Baba, Meher. God Speaks. Dodd Mead, 1997.

Carlson, Richard. Don't Sweat the Small Stuff. Hyperion, 1996.

Dunn, Jean. Prior to Consciousness. Acorn, 1990.

Godman, David. Be As You Are: The Teachings of Sri Ramana Maharshi. Arkana, 1985.

Godman, David. Nothing Ever Happened. Avadhuta Foundation, 1998.

Hay, Louise. You Can Heal Your Life. Hay House, 1999.

Holt, Jim. Why Does the World Exist. Liveright, 2012.

Keating, Thomas. Open Mind, Open Heart: The Contemplative Dimension of the Gospel. Continuum International Publishing Group, 1994.

Klein, Jean. Be Who You Are. Non-Duality Press, 2006.

Klein, Jean. I Am. Non-Duality Press, 2006.

Krishnamurti, Jiddu. The Awakening of Intelligence. Harper & Row, 1987.

Maharaj, Nisargadatta. I Am That. Acorn, 2012.

Maharshi, Ramana. Talks With Ramana Maharshi: On Realizing Abiding Peace and Happiness. Inner Directions, 2000.

Yogananda, Paramahansa. Autobiography of a Yogi. Self Realization Fellowship, 2007.

ACKNOWLEDGMENTS

I would like to thank my daughters, Mariah and Ailee, for taking some time to read the manuscript and for their many helpful suggestions. Thank you, girls. Love you, madly. Madly love this whole female family!

I would especially like to express gratitude to my friend, Jane Blake, for also reading the manuscript with an unerring editorial eye that guided its composition so much for the better, and for the hours of conversation that contributed to many of its ideas. Thank you, Jane. You're a Master!

ABOUT THE AUTHOR

A child of Holocaust survivors - his father fought in the Warsaw ghetto uprising - Solomon Katz was reared in classical Judaism and was fluent in biblical Hebrew at an early age. He majored in philosophy - especially Indian philosophy - at SUNY Stony Brook. After graduating, he joined the Lindisfarne spiritual community then at Southampton, Long Island. At Lindisfarne he was introduced to Zen, Yoga, and Vipassana (Insight) meditation. His interest in meditation eventually led him to Asia, where he lived as a Buddhist monk and meditation teacher in Burma and Sri Lanka. In Sri Lanka, he lived for a while in the hermitage at Salgala, on top of a mountain jutting out of the rainforest, where a group of gray langurs, a cobra, and iguana were his closest neighbors; and he taught meditation at Kanduboda. By the time he returned West and began a doctoral program at Harvard University, he had spent three full years in periods (three months here, six months there) of silent meditation. At Harvard, he earned concurrent graduate degrees in Religions of the World (M.T.S.), and in Counseling and Consulting Psychology (M.Ed., Ed.D.). He trained in, practiced, and taught psychology at Mt. Auburn Hospital, a Harvard affiliated teaching hospital, and held a faculty position as Clinical Instructor in Psychology at Harvard Medical School. During this twenty year span at Harvard, he also married, raised four daughters and, now with an empty nest, is presenting this book of wisdom gleaned from his extensive meditative, academic and clinical experience.

Made in the USA
San Bernardino, CA
08 March 2020

65439985R00168